READING
REASONS

READING REASONS

Motivational Mini-Lessons for Middle and High School

Kelly Gallagher

Stenhouse Publishers
Portland, Maine

Stenhouse Publishers
www.stenhouse.com

Credits

Library of Congress Cataloging-in-Publication Data
Gallagher, Kelly, 1958–
    Reading reasons : motivational mini-lessons for middle and high school / Kelly Gallagher.
    p. cm.
    Includes bibliographical references.
    ISBN 1-57110-356-2 (alk. paper)
    1. Reading (Secondary). I. Title.
LB1632.G35 2003
428.4'071'2—dc21   2002042775

Cover photography by Jim Arbogast/Getty Images

Manufactured in the United States of America on acid-free paper
09 08   9 8 7

For Kristin, Caitlin, and Devin
"Mucher than much . . ."

CONTENTS

List of the Forty Mini-Lessons   ix

Acknowledgments   xi

Introduction: "Why Should I Read?"   1

1 Our Greatest Challenge   3

2 The Nine Reading Reasons   15

3 The Forty Mini-Lessons   39

4 Developing Your Own Reading Reason Lens   139

Appendixes A–K   151

Bibliography   179

LIST OF THE FORTY MINI-LESSONS

1. **Reading Is Rewarding**   **41**
   Favorite First Lines   42
   The Reading Minute   44
   Reading Wisdom   46
   Who Lives in Your House?   48

2. **Reading Builds a Mature Vocabulary**   **51**
   Brain Food   52
   Building Your Vocabulary   54
   Don't Be Such a Borf!   56
   Word Attack!   58

3. **Reading Makes You a Better Writer**   **61**
   Cooking Up Good Writing   62
   Reading as a Writing Model   64
   Says Who?   66
   Slim Shadings   68

4. **Reading Is Hard, and "Hard" Is Necessary**   **71**
   Driving Good Reading   72
   An Educated Electorate   74
   The Fine Print   76
   Phone Home   78
   Reading the World   80
   Uncle Sam Wants You!   82
   You Are What You Eat   84

5. **Reading Makes You Smarter**   **87**
   Brain Maintenance   88
   Join the Million Word Club   90
   Read All About It!   92

Rustproofing   94
Who Scores Highest?   96

6. **Reading Prepares You for the World of Work**   **99**
   Get a Job!   100
   Reading Demands of the Workplace   102
   Reading Is Job One   104
   Sharpening Work Skills   106

7. **Reading Well Is Financially Rewarding**   **109**
   How Much Will You Be Paid for Attending Class Today?   110
   Making Bank   112
   Nerds Win   114
   Raising a Child   116

8. **Reading Opens the Door to College and Beyond**   **119**
   Getting in College Reading Shape   120
   The Key to College   122
   The Road to Higher Learning   124
   Survival of the Fittest   126

9. **Reading Arms You Against Oppression**   **129**
   Bridging the Digital Divide   130
   Closing the Achievement Gap   132
   Fighting Poverty   134
   The More You Know . . .   136

ACKNOWLEDGMENTS

My heartfelt thanks go to Bill Varner, my editor at Stenhouse, for his kindness, guidance, and support. Because of his editing abilities, the book in your hand is much better than the one I originally wrote. Many thanks to Martha Drury, as well, for her production expertise. I hope she is not waking at night dreaming of formatting mini-lessons. Thanks also to Philippa, Tom, and all the staff at Stenhouse for their support.

Thanks to Sharon Qualls and Sheri Krumins for allowing me access to their reading classes to test-drive many of these Reading Reasons.

I would also like to thank the following great teachers, all of whom have played a large role in my professional, and often personal, development:

John Powers, for putting up with all those nagging questions during our carpool rides. Though you are mistaken about the Kennedy assassination, you have greatly shaped my thinking about teaching. Thank you.

Mary K. Healy, for showing me what great teaching looks like. You were the first person I told that I was going to attempt to write a book. You did not laugh. That meant a great deal to me.

Liz Simons, for bringing me into the Puente Project, and for always addressing the student question "Why should I care?" I am one of you, forever.

Jeff McQuillan, for your encouragement that I could actually pull this off. That lunch meeting was the motivation I needed. You don't know how comforting it is to have a voice of reason out there.

Joe Calwell, for modeling great passion in your teaching, year in and year out. It is no accident that former students from years ago still write you. I wish you well in your retirement. Your influence persists.

Carol Jago, for taking a young teacher and filling his head with possibilities in the early days of the California Reading and Literature Project at UCLA.

Kathy Schymick, for a distinguished career turning adolescents into readers. Don't forget: you still owe me one.

And last, but not least, to my mom—thanks for the teaching gene.

INTRODUCTION: "WHY SHOULD I READ?"

Not long ago I escorted a ninth-grade class to the school library with directions that every student was to check out a book by the end of the period. After a brief tour of the various sections and a lesson on how to locate titles, authors, and genres, the students were given forty minutes to make their selections. Because it was the beginning of a new year and I was interested in getting them started as readers, I asked the students to choose something they would enjoy reading—something recreational, rather than academic, in nature.

Some students (most likely those who were already readers) found books quickly. Others took more time, perusing a number of books before deciding on titles they could live with. As the period progressed, students who had made their choices sat down and began reading. With five minutes to go, I noticed one student, Richard, still searching for a book.

Richard considered and returned at least twenty books to the shelves during our short visit to the library. Nothing looked good to him. I quietly approached him and tried to find out what his interests were. Richard told me he liked baseball, so we located a small section of baseball books. As Richard and I looked at every baseball book in the library collection, and as he rejected each of them one by one, I could see his frustration mounting. Standing in that library and looking at the sour look on Richard's face, one might have thought that instead of choosing a book I had asked him to don an orange vest and spend his school year collecting trash along the highway. After rejecting the last baseball title on the shelf, Richard, in exasperation, turned to me and said, "I like baseball, but I don't like to read. Reading is boring and pointless. Why should I read?"

Have you ever been asked a question that has so many obvious answers that you have difficulty formulating any answer at all? "Why should I read?" is that kind of question for me. When Richard asked me that question, so many possible answers ran simultaneously through my mind that a sort of rush-hour gridlock ground all my responses to a halt. In trying to decide which answer was the best to start with, my brain became as jammed as a Toys "R" Us parking lot three days before Christmas. Having only a minute remaining in the class period did not help matters. How does one even begin to suggest the depth and richness to be had from reading? Ask Julia Child why she cooks or Yo-Yo Ma why he plays the cello and see if they can answer in a minute or less.

When my last class left that day, I sat down and, with Richard in mind, jotted down all the reasons why I read. The next day, I asked the class to do the same. As a group, we brainstormed all the reasons we should be readers. I wrote their reasons on an overhead transparency; and, after some revising and regrouping, a list of nine major reasons why we should all be readers emerged. I proposed to the students that we repeatedly revisit each of these reasons as the year progressed, and I told them I would share any research I came across to validate their reading reasons.

Thus a journey to explore answers to the question "Why should I read?" began. I wanted answers that adolescents would find meaningful. Answers that would resonate with my students. Answers that would allow them to see the importance reading has in the lives of literate people. Answers they could internalize and believe in long after leaving my class.

I didn't know it at the time, but that day was the genesis of this book. A quest for reading reasons had begun.

1

OUR GREATEST CHALLENGE

If you make a student feel like a reader, he'll become a reader.

Donald Graves

Here is a fantasy of mine: it's the first day of the school year and I'm standing at my classroom door greeting my new students:

"Good morning, Maria. I understand you have read twenty-seven books this summer. Welcome to my class! Come in! Let's meet at lunch later this week so I can hear your thoughts on why Hamlet waited so long to exact his revenge.

"Michael, I'm sorry, but I have heard from your previous teachers that you are an unmotivated reader. Unfortunately, I'm not allowing any student to enroll in my classroom this year until he demonstrates he has discovered the joys and wonders of reading. Please go see your counselor for a class change. You may reenroll when you've become a lifelong learner.

"Hi, you must be Nadia. Your older sister told me you are a semi-motivated reader. I will allow you to enroll in the class, but you will remain on a probationary basis until you demonstrate ownership of your education. If you make meaningful strides toward becoming an intrinsically motivated reader, I'll allow you to stay in the class. Please have a seat."

Absurd, I know. We are not given license to stand at the threshold of our classrooms and accept only those students who have already developed a passion for reading—nor, frankly, would I want to. In reality, we know our new students will be bringing with them a wide range of reading abilities and attitudes, and it will be our task—our charge—in the next 180 school days to help them develop as readers. Therein lies one of our greatest challenges: good readers or poor, voracious or reluctant, fluent or slow, it is our responsibility to make all our students feel like readers, to make our students become readers, and to make our students remain readers long after they have left our schools. A daunting thought; but if we don't accept this challenge, who will?

As teachers, we want all our students to lead lives in which reading matters. Further, we want students to become many kinds of readers—readers of academic text, readers of functional or "real world" print, and readers of recreational materials. This is a lofty goal, given that many of our students enter our doors as inexperienced, aliterate, or nonexistent readers. Some arrive from homes and apartments devoid of reading materials—no books, no newspapers, no magazines, no Internet. But a lack of access to books isn't always the reason for students' not reading. Many of my students have books at home, but for one reason or another, reading hasn't assumed a prominent role in their lives. For a myriad of reasons, they come to class the first day of school not having read a single book over summer vacation. The idea of reading for pleasure, of reading when it is not assigned, is foreign to them. This is always a shock to English teachers, who treasure summer as an opportunity to catch up on all the neglected reading piled up on their nightstands.

But the problems we teachers face reach far beyond the world of recreational reading. We are increasingly seeing students who, when confronted with challenging assigned reading (a biology textbook, a state-mandated exam, or some other difficult material), often give up easily. They are unable, or unwilling, to tackle difficult text. In short, they are not in reading "shape." This raises serious questions for teachers. How do we turn around this apathy? How do we address this unwillingness to read? How do we light a reading fire under our students? How do we shelter fragile adolescent readers and help them grow into people for whom reading matters? How can we meaningfully and consistently reinforce the benefits of reading? Where do we start?

Building Readers

Occasionally I'll be at a workshop and a colleague, usually a newer teacher who has heard that I've had some success motivating my students to read, will pull me aside and ask me the million-dollar question: How do I get my reluctant teenagers to read? The teacher then stands there, awaiting my quick response, expecting some magical pearl of wisdom to spill out of me, which will thus inspire an instantaneous transformation in the reading lives of that teacher's students. The truth is that there is no single, quick answer. If there were, the problem of motivating students to read more wouldn't be as widespread.

Building reading motivation requires complex construction. There isn't a single right motivational tool. What inspires one student to read might not move another. We therefore cannot use the same approach with every student. To maximize our chances of success, we need to sell students on a wide range of reasons why they should read. These reasons—lots of them—need to be made visible to our students. They should be shared early and often, and repeated and overlapped to construct a strong foundation of reading motivation. Each reason does not stand alone; rather, they build upon each other and strengthen one another. No single reason will turn around a reluctant reader. But together, over the course of a school year, many reasons send the message that reading is rewarding. The number, strength, and diversity of the reasons presented in this book build a compelling case for reading.

To maximize the effectiveness of these reading reasons, however, certain building blocks must be in place.

Building Block 1: Students need access to high-interest reading materials.

My first year in the classroom I was hired to teach five periods of high school remedial reading. There was one minor hitch: not a single book could be found in my assigned classroom. I am not exaggerating. There was not one book. Instead, the retiring teacher bequeathed to me three mammoth file cabinets. Inside were 180 folders, one for each day of the year, each holding a worksheet-of-the-day. And we wonder why most students never make it out of the remedial track.

Recognizing the absurdity of trying to teach adolescents to become readers without having books at my disposal, I regularly set aside class time to take students to the library. I insisted that students leave the library at the end of each visit with books in their possession. I was successful at getting students to check out many books, but I was not very successful at turning these students into readers. There is something about a teacher's mandating a library visit that reeks of coercion. Sure, students were checking out books, but many were doing so because *I* wanted them to, not because *they* were motivated to read. In short, it was just another assignment to fulfill in order to make the teacher happy or to earn the desired grade. My students' motivation was extrinsic.

Fifteen years later, my students now read many times more books than my students did during my first year. What's the key difference? What accounts for this surge in reading? Far and away the most important factor was the establishment of a classroom library. I brought interesting books to my students. I surrounded them with a variety of high-interest reading materials. I now have 2,500 books in my classroom, and I am convinced that developing this "book flood" (a phrase coined by New Zealand researcher Warwick Elley) is the single most important thing I have done in my teaching career. My classroom library is stocked with high-interest adolescent reading materials of all shapes, sizes, levels, and genres, from comic books to Shakespeare, from picture books to Sigmund Freud. (For high-interest adolescent reading titles, see Appendix B, "101 Books Every Classroom Library Should Have.") It's true that some of these books are also available in the school library, but something powerful happens when books are brought to the students, when teachers take time to talk the books up, when students are immersed daily in print. Jeff McQuillan, in *The Literacy Crisis*, makes a strong case with a simple equation:

more books = more reading = better reading

In *Teaching Reading in High School English Classes* (Ericson 2001), McQuillan writes of a book flood experiment he and other teachers developed in an urban, lower socioeconomic school. The teachers surrounded their non-reading students with high-interest reading materials for a year. The result? By the end of the second semester, teachers reported significant growth in students' fluency, comprehension, and—perhaps most important—enjoyment of reading. Most of the students began the year with a negative view of reading, but "by the end of the first semester almost all of the students had read several books on their own, and continued to read throughout the school year" (p. 79). McQuillan's experiment gave credence to something I've always suspected: all students like to read; they just don't all know it yet.

As you consider the motivational mini-lessons found in this book, remember the importance of surrounding your students with interesting things to read. Just as you can't golf without clubs or paint without a brush, you can't become a reader without good books (the American Library Association recommends that there be 1,500 books in every classroom—see Appendix A for the Three Commandments of Classroom Libraries). The motivation strategies in this book are most effective when students have access to interesting reading material.

Building Block 2: Students must have a time to read and a place to read.

Putting good books in the hands of a student is crucial, but will do very little good unless the student has a time and a place to read. Some of our students have time to read at home, but no place to do so; others have a place, but no time. For many students, school is the only place where the three key factors merge: having a book to read, a place to read, and time to read.

If we accept the premise that one becomes a better reader by reading, then we should be alarmed at how little time our students spend actually reading. Many studies have indicated that the amount of reading done by students peaks around the fifth grade, and by junior and senior high school the reading done by students drops off precipitously. In his research, Terrence Paul found the following:

- The average amount of time spent reading for all grades is 7.1 minutes a day in public schools around the nation.
- The peak reading years are the fourth and fifth grades. By the time students reach high school, they are spending about as much time on literature-based reading as kindergartners.
- Students in the top 5 percent of national reading scores read 144 times more than students in the bottom 5 percent.
- Students in the highest-performing states in the National Assessment of Educational Progress (NAEP) reading study engaged in 59 percent more reading than those in states in the bottom quartile.

The evidence is compelling that our students are not doing enough reading, both inside school and out. This raises two questions: 1) In the midst of daily lectures, group work, and essay writing, am I carving out enough valuable curricular time *in class* for students to actually read? 2) When the last bell of the day rings and the students leave campus, am I putting too much faith in my reluctant readers to believe that actual reading practice is occurring at home?

Consider this scenario: your school hires you to be the head basketball coach and charges you with the task of producing the best basketball players possible. You would probably begin by identifying the areas of greatest need and design practices to meet those needs. To teach players the necessary skills, you would conduct thorough practices under your direct supervision. You would not leave anything to chance. It would be ludicrous, therefore, for a varsity coach to address his team as follows: "As we prepare for the big game Friday night, I will not be conducting any practices at school. Instead, I want you to go home and practice on your own for a number of hours to improve your skills. Good luck, don't cut any corners, and I'll see you at the game Friday night." This probably wouldn't present any problems for "gym rats," players who already love to play basketball, but do you think the students who dislike basketball will go home and vigorously practice alone every night? Highly doubtful. Yet isn't this the approach we often take with reluctant readers? We tell them that lots of reading is good for them and that they should go home and do lots of it. Some do, but the ones who need it the most often do not.

The most successful basketball players, like the best readers, do both, of course. They work hard under the auspices of a coach, and they motivate themselves to practice on their own. A good player doesn't rely on one or the other. (Michael Jordan spent thousands of hours practicing outside of the team's scheduled practices.) If one improves reading by reading, then it follows that time must be set aside during the school day to ensure that reading takes place, and it also follows that we have to maintain high expectations that students will do a heavy amount of reading at home. It should not be one or the other. Both expectations, reading at school and at home, are essential to building readers. (In the Anaheim Union High School District, where I work, sustained silent reading—SSR—has been implemented campuswide at every one of our eighteen schools, thus ensuring that our students have time for daily reading practice. It helps to have a superintendent who is a former English teacher.)

Time spent reading, during SSR and otherwise, also correlates strongly with higher test scores. In a study of fifth graders, Richard Anderson, Paul Wilson, and Linda Fielding found that the more students read, the higher they scored on standardized reading exams. Conversely, the less students read, the lower they scored. The correlation, as noted in the following table, was strong:

Percentile Rank	Minutes of Text Reading per Day	Estimated Number of Words Read per Year
98	90.7	4,733,000
90	40.4	2,357,000
70	21.7	1,168,000
50	12.9	601,000
20	3.1	134,000
10	1.6	51,000

The researchers found that students who scored in the 98th percentile read on the average of ninety minutes a day, which translates to reading nearly five million words a year. If a student reads almost five million words a year, he or she is going to score well on any reading assessment. Students who read infrequently, however, scored very poorly. Though the researchers were measuring fifth graders, I have found this ratio of reading time to number of words read to be an accurate rate for my high school readers. This study argues forcefully for the importance of setting aside time and a place for students to read, especially in this age of state and national testing.

Building Block 3: Teachers must model the value of reading.

In the fall of 1993, I decided to launch a faculty book club at the high school where I taught in Anaheim. The premise of the club was simple: interested teachers would select a title, go out and read it, and meet on the last Friday of the month during lunch to informally discuss the book. I set a date for the first meeting, printed fliers and placed them in the faculty mailboxes, put messages in the faculty bulletin, purchased copies of the first selection in advance, and waited for the teachers to stampede my room for the first meeting. Only four (out of seventy-five) teachers showed up.

Why only four teachers? What was the problem? The problem was that our teachers, like all teachers, were buried under the demands of teaching. Planning lessons, grading essays, completing paperwork, conferring with students and parents, serving on committees, and attending dances, concerts, plays, and sporting events cut into reading time. The demands of teaching had created a roadblock to the library and bookstore.

This was understandable, but our lack of reading was creating a credibility problem with our students. How could we sell kids on the value of reading when we teachers were not reading? Students are quick to notice such hypocrisy. Realizing this, I had established the faculty book club in an attempt to motivate teachers (including myself) to rediscover reading. Knowing that other teachers would be reading the same book and would be counting on me to participate in a discussion encouraged me to set aside time (mostly television time) in my hectic day to read. Even though only four teachers showed up for that first meeting, we forged ahead.

Slowly but surely, word began to spread, and we started to gain more faculty members. Implementing a schoolwide SSR program helped tremendously. Today, nine years later, the Magnolia High School Faculty Book Club has a membership of thirty-three teachers across the content areas. To date we have read eighty books (see Appendix G for a full listing).

The faculty book club has changed the reading culture of Magnolia High School. It has reignited reading among teachers, fostered collegiality among faculty and staff, and allowed teacher-readers to lead students by example. Most important, it has conveyed the message to students that reading is important in our lives and books are something to get excited about. The list in Appendix G is posted in my classroom so that students see me as an active reader. Worksheets and computers do not instill a reading habit in our students; teachers leading by example do. (See Appendix C for monthly motivational ideas.)

Conversely, teachers who grade papers or balance their checkbooks during SSR time are also sending their students a powerful message—a message that time set aside to read isn't important. It's true that we often have to model a positive behavior ten, twenty, thirty times before we see it begin to take hold in adolescents. But it's also true that if we model a bad behavior *once*, they learn it immediately. I remind myself of this prior to every SSR period—that as a teacher I am more influential as a model than my students will ever let on. If I talk the talk, I need to walk the walk.

Building Block 4: Teachers must stop grading everything.

Picture yourself during spring break at some far-off exotic beach location. There is not a cell phone, pager, computer, or school intercom in sight. You are the only soul on the pristine beach, which is chamber-of-commerce, postcard perfect. The concept of "teenager" has faded into the deep recesses of your brain. You have worked hard for this break, a respite you richly deserve. You have brought with you something deliciously trashy to read, a guilty pleasure you have saved for this moment. You plant your beach chair in the soft, powdery sand and crack your just-for-fun book, not a worry on the horizon. As you relax and begin to get into the first chapter, you are suddenly and rudely interrupted by the appearance of a dreaded former English teacher who suddenly sneaks up behind you and says, "I love that book you're reading! Let me grade your comprehension as you read it! Since it may take you a few hours to finish, I'll return every half hour or so and drop a pop quiz on you. When you're finished with the book, I'll give you an exam to see how well you understood it. After that, you can make a diorama to illustrate your favorite scene. But, hey, for now, don't worry about it—go ahead and enjoy!"

My guess is that any enjoyment you might have had from reading that book just evaporated. The very notion that someone wants to assess your recreational reading is counterproductive to your purpose: to enjoy reading. As this example illustrates, there are times when assessment is beneficial and there are times when it is harmful. I learned some time ago that if I want to develop a love of recreational reading in my students, I have to resist the urge to grade everything they read.

Similarly, we can learn this lesson of not grading all reading assignments in the paradox we face when teaching students how to improve their writing. The writing Catch-22 goes something like this:

- Students' writing will improve only if they write a lot.
- Students' writing will improve only if they receive some meaningful feedback on their writing.
- Responding meaningfully to all the students' papers takes a lot of time.

- If grading takes a long time, students will wait longer between writing assignments.
- If students wait longer between writing assignments, they will not be doing enough writing to improve.

The solution (more writing) creates a problem (more grading) that prevents the solution (more writing). The only way around this paradox is for me to accept the notion that my students will simply have to write more than I can grade. They will still receive meaningful feedback, though not on every assignment. I will have to utilize peer responses and read-around groups. They will not sit around waiting for me to grade everything before they write more. As a general rule of thumb, I ask my students to write four times more than I can grade. I explain to them (and their parents) that if they don't write this much, they will not get enough practice to improve their craft.

If I accept the notion that students will not develop as writers unless they write much more than I can grade, then it makes sense that they will not develop as readers unless they read a lot more than I can grade as well. I have to accept the notion that they should read much more than I can assess. Students are evaluated enough when it comes to academic reading. If I want them to become lifelong recreational readers, I need to let go of my desire to grade everything, particularly if I am trying to get them to see that reading is fun. I need to stop being the English teacher sneaking up behind my students on the beach with the pop quiz in hand.

Building Block 5: Teachers must provide structure to a reading program.

Though I don't assess much of my students' pleasure reading, I do have them keep track of everything (academic, recreational, functional) they read on both a Reading Log (see Appendix H) and a Reading Record, adapted from Nancie Atwell's *In the Middle* (see Appendix I). These forms are used to measure whether students are meeting the independent reading expectations of my school district, which are as follows:

Grade level	Number of words read in a year	Number of pages read in a month	Time spent reading in a year
Grade 7	1,000,000	200-page book a month	60 hours
Grade 8	1,000,000	200-page book a month	60 hours
Grade 9	1,250,000	250-page book a month	75 hours
Grade 10	1,500,000	300-page book a month	90 hours
Grade 11	1,750,000	350-page book a month	105 hours
Grade 12	2,000,000	400-page book a month	120 hours

The Reading Log is used to track daily independent reading assignments and total time spent reading. This log is for independent reading only. It does not apply to any teacher-assigned reading. Students fill in the form anytime they read independently outside the school walls. They mark the date and indicate what they read by marking "B" for book, "N" for newspaper, "M" for magazine, or "O" for other (e.g., Internet, comic books). There is a line available for a one-sentence description of what they read. They complete the log by indicating how long they read and totaling their running reading time. On Friday they take the log home for the weekend, draw a line under their week's reading with a highlighter, and have a parent sign the highlighted area. They then return the logs on Monday and we continue tracking our time. Their overall time is tracked in class using the chart found in Appendix K. To keep students honest, I reserve the right to meet with them at random and ask questions about their reading.

The Reading Record is used to keep track of all the works students have read (or abandoned). It provides a record of all kinds of reading the student might do, from academic to recreational. Periodicals are not included; the Reading Record is reserved for large works (books and plays) only. The idea is to encourage students to move beyond magazine reading, to become readers of books. Every student in my school district has a Reading Record, printed on heavy stock for durability. This record follows the student from grade to grade.

Having students track their reading on both a daily and a yearly basis serves as a reminder that they are progressing as readers. The Reading Record and Reading Log are not graded, but they are prerequisites for obtaining specific grades in the class. For example, to receive an A in the class, a student must meet three requirements: 1) he or she must earn an A average on all graded assignments; 2) he or she must read 120 hours; and 3) he or she must read twelve major works, both academic and recreational, some assigned, some free choice. Only the first criteria is graded; the other two are prerequisites. In other words, a student who earns an A on all the graded assignments will only keep that grade if he or she has met the reading requirements. Otherwise, the student earns a lower grade. This is true at each grade point; each has graduated requirements.

Establishing a high reading target is important. As the old saying goes, "No one rises to low expectations." Having students chart their reading progress enables them to recognize their advancement as readers.

Why Before How

These five building blocks—allowing more access to reading, providing a time and place, modeling the value of reading, placing less emphasis on grading, and providing structure to measure progress—work in concert with one another. They are effective only when they are applied simultaneously, when they are visited and revisited, when they overlap. Alone, each is ineffective. Together, they form the necessary foundation for building adolescent readers.

There is, however, one element still missing—an element far too frequently overlooked when considering how to turn children on to reading: motivation.

Building Block 6: Students must want to read—they must see what's in it for them.

We spend a lot of time in education discussing *how* to get students to be better readers. We don't spend enough time, in my view, on sharing with students *why* they should become readers.

Let's say you decide one day that you'd like to be a competitive swimmer. Even if you are the most motivated student in aquatic history, it is safe to say that you will not develop without some critical factors: a pool to practice in, a coach to point you in the right direction, and lots of practice time. Similarly, you could not become an excellent tennis player unless you had a racket, an available court, coaching, and—again—lots of time to practice. Whether it's swimming or tennis, having access to the right equipment, sound coaching, and extensive practice time are nonnegotiable prerequisites.

But it takes more than that. Before anything else, you must be motivated. You can have an Olympic-size pool in your backyard, a gold-medal-winning coach, and ample practice time, but you won't develop into a competitive swimmer unless you have the *desire* to be a competitive swimmer. You have to see the value in getting in that pool every day. You have to *want* to swim. You need to be convinced that swimming every day is worthwhile, not because someone else wants you to be a great swimmer, but because you see the value in it yourself. The payoff, you feel, is worth it.

The same is true of reading. Students must want to become better readers, not because someone else wants them to, but because the rewards of reading have been made visible to them. The value of reading must become internalized. This does not happen by osmosis. Students must be led to it. I learned this during my sophomore year in high school.

As a high school student, I liked to read, but I did not care for poetry. My English teacher confessed to the class that she didn't like poetry either, but felt obligated to "expose" us to it because poetry was a required unit in the tenth-grade curriculum. Thus, I began my first foray into poetry with two strikes against me: I didn't like poetry and neither did my teacher. Not surprisingly, I graduated from high school with the notion that poetry was boring and meaningless.

A couple of years later, much to my dismay, I found myself studying poetry in a college course. Prepared to hate poetry once again, I gradually underwent an unexpected transformation. Through the enthusiasm and guidance of my professor, I began to see the beauty of poetry. I gained an appreciation of the power of rhythm, the importance of sound, the craft of economy. I learned to love the rules (iambic pentameter) and the lack of rules (free verse). I liked the playfulness and the seriousness of it. By the end of the semester, I had come to realize how wrongheaded I had been about poetry. I had undergone an intellectual makeover, if you will, and a poetry reader was born.

What's the point of this anecdote? Today I love nothing better than to read a poem by Jimmy Santiago Baca, Charles Bukowski, or Czeslaw Milosz. I have discovered that the poetry section of the bookstore is a good place to get lost for an hour. I don't need anyone to tell me that poetry is good for me and that I should read it once in a while. I have become a poetry reader—it is now intrinsic with me. Poetry matters to me.

But this appreciation, this acquiring of a poetry habit, would never have happened had I not been shown the way by a gifted teacher. There was a transitional phase in which I was led to that appreciation. Frankly, I had to be sold on the idea of poetry, but once I was, I gained ownership of the appreciation. Had I not been sold (extrinsic) on the worth of poetry, I would never have acquired an appreciation of that worth (intrinsic). My high school teacher's inability to get me to see the pleasure and value of poetry did not give me a fighting chance to acquire a poetry habit on my own. Surrounding me with poems in high school wasn't enough. I needed a push (more like a shove) in the right direction in order for the beauty of poetry to take hold. I was convinced I did not like poetry. I was wrong.

We must prove to our nonreaders they are wrong about reading. Students are human and, being human, seek pleasure or value. Like most people, their first thought will be, "What's in it for me?" Unfortunately, many of our students see reading as just another assignment, something generated by the teacher. We must prove otherwise by demonstrating to our students that reading is worthwhile and show them that there is a world of reward in it for them. In a way, by providing these six foundational blocks we are providing reading training wheels. If we are successful, eventually the wheels will be removed and students will ride away, self-propelled readers.

2

THE NINE
READING REASONS

A good teacher can influence even the most unpromising of students to the unique strength of his or her own mind.

Lewis H. Lapham

When my daughter was in the third grade, she rushed home one day, excited about a new reading program at her school. The program, called "Book It!," offered any student who read three books free pizza at a local pizza parlor. All she had to do was read three books, have a parent sign a card vouching for her, and a steaming piece of pepperoni pizza was promised for her immediate future. The program had its intended effect. She came home that day fired up to read. What could possibly be wrong with that?

Plenty. The first thing she did was dig through the books in her room to grab the three shortest books she could find. If she hurried, she reasoned, we could possibly venture to the pizza parlor that night! It didn't matter that she had already read these books and that none of them were particular favorites of hers. Visions of deep-pan pepperoni had possessed her.

What bothered me the most was the message this program was sending my daughter. It was telling her that the act of reading itself, the pleasure of a great book, was not enough inducement to become a reader. Rather, it suggested that reading is such a chore that we need to offer rewards, or bribes, to get you to do it. Alfie Kohn, in his book *Punished by Rewards,* argues convincingly that in the long run rewards actually de-motivate our students. We have become a nation, Kohn argues, far too overreliant on offering extrinsic rewards for tasks that are intrinsically rewarding. If I tell my young daughter she will get a dish of ice cream if she first eats her broccoli, she'll probably eat it. However, the chances that she will be eating broccoli twenty years from now will be diminished because of the bribe I'm offering her. If I give her pizza or some other reward for reading, what is the real message I'm sending about reading? If programs like Book It! catch fire, Kohn surmises, we might develop into a nation of overweight people who dislike reading.

By the time many of our students come to us from elementary school, they have been bribed and rewarded so frequently that they have forgotten the best reasons to read. The act of reading just for the pleasure of it has been buried under stickers, candies, and other bribes. The problem, as Book It! illustrates, is that many students come to us without any intrinsic motivation to read. They often have little or no concept of the beauty of the written word, nor do they see the necessity of honing their reading skills in the dawn of a new information age. They don't understand that reading is power, and that by becoming proficient, self-motivated readers they arm themselves against injustice and hegemony. They do not readily comprehend that the ability to read a book critically gives them the cognitive underpinnings to read the world (a politician, an advertisement) critically. They don't understand that the act of reading makes them better readers and writers. They're oblivious to the latest brain research, which suggests that reading opens neurological pathways (in layman's terms: reading makes you smarter) and that the act of reading helps to keep your mind sharp as you age.

We adults recognize all of these reasons, but for one reason or another we have done an expert job of keeping them a secret from our students. These reasons have become second nature to us—so much so that we often erroneously assume that our students are aware of them as well. We have become stealth readers in front of a generation of students starving to see these reading reasons modeled.

This book is about uncovering and sharing these intrinsic reading "secrets" with our students. It's about making the invisible visible. Like my poetry professor, I will show my students the beauty and value of reading. If I'm successful, I trust this beauty and value will take hold in their lives. Like it did in mine. Like it did in yours.

"Why Should I Read?"

Getting students to start reading in September is only the first part of the problem facing junior and senior high school teachers. The genesis of this book was born out of the frustration I felt watching my students' initial reading enthusiasm wane as the year progressed. Much like a marathon, the school year is long and pace is needed. Many of my students, good readers or not, often "hit the wall" in November, or February, or May. The reasons why they should read, which were clearly articulated and motivated students to start reading in the fall, are often forgotten by springtime.

Students need scheduled reading "booster shots" to help revisit the question "Why should I read?" on a regular basis. To do this effectively, teachers need to be armed with a series of short mini-lessons, ranging from five to twenty minutes in length, that will help them make the benefits of reading visible. These mini-lessons, based on the nine reading reasons outlined in the balance of this chapter, will help you create and maintain a high level of student reading motivation, not just in the fall, but throughout the school year.

Three years ago I began spending the first few minutes of class every Thursday sharing with students a different reason why they should read. Students kept a record of all the mini-lessons in their reader's notebooks. Near the end of the year I had them reflect on all the reading reasons and asked them to try to categorize them. After much discussion and a bit of negotiation, the students decided there were nine major reasons to read.

We should read because:

1. Reading is rewarding.
2. Reading builds a mature vocabulary.
3. Reading makes you a better writer.
4. Reading is hard, and "hard" is necessary.
5. Reading makes you smarter.
6. Reading prepares you for the world of work.
7. Reading well is financially rewarding.
8. Reading opens the door to college and beyond.
9. Reading arms you against oppression.

Let's take a closer look at each of these reasons.

Reason 1: Reading Is Rewarding

I became an English teacher in part because I love to read. Even after fifteen years of teaching, I love being the person who introduces my students to Atticus Finch, Winston Smith, Dr. Jekyll and Mr. Hyde, and Romeo and Juliet. Better yet, I'm paid to do this! I'm guessing that many of you reading this book feel the same way. Books are lifeblood to us, and we can't fathom a world without them. Anne Lamott, in *Bird by Bird,* captures this sentiment eloquently:

> For some of us, books are as important as almost anything else on Earth. What a miracle it is that out of these small, flat, rigid squares of paper unfolds world after world after world, worlds that sing to you, comfort and quiet or excite you. Books help us understand who we are and how we are to behave. They show us what community and friendship mean; they show us how to live and how to die. They are full of all the things you don't get in real life— wonderful, lyrical language, for instance, right off the bat. And quality of attention: we may notice amazing details during the course of the day but we rarely let ourselves stop and pay attention. An author makes you notice, makes you pay attention, and this is a great gift. My gratitude for good writing is unbounded; I'm grateful for it the way I'm grateful for the ocean. Aren't you? I ask. (p. 15)

When we discover this fine, lyrical language Lamott speaks of, it is imperative that we bring it into the classroom to share with our students. For some time we teachers have understood that if we want our students to write the best possible essays we need to show them models of great writing. Shouldn't the same idea hold true for reading as well? Bringing excellent examples of reading to our students will help develop their sensibilities as readers. We need to bring them great passages, like this one from Laura Hillenbrand's *Seabiscuit: An American Legend,* which describes what it is like to sit atop a horse as it is racing:

A Thoroughbred horse is one of God's most impressive engines. Tipping the scales at up to 1,450 pounds, he can sustain speeds of forty miles per hour. Equipped with reflexes must faster than those of the most quick-wired man, he swoops over as much as twenty-eight feet of earth in a single stride, and corners on a dime. His body is a paradox of mass and lightness, crafted to slip through air with the ease of an arrow. His mind is impressed with a single command: run. He pursues speed with superlative courage, pushing beyond defeat, beyond exhaustion, sometimes beyond the structural limits of bone and sinew. In flight, he's nature's ultimate wedding of form and purpose.

To pilot a racehorse is to ride a half-ton catapult. It is without question one of the most formidable feats in sport. The extraordinary athleticism of the jockey is unparalleled: A study of the elements of athleticism conducted by Los Angeles exercise physiologists and physicians found that of all major sport competitors, jockeys may be, pound for pound, the best overall athletes. They have to be. To begin with, there are demands on balance, coordination, reflex. A horse's body is a constantly shifting topography, with a bobbing head and neck and roiling muscle over the shoulders, back, and rump. On a running horse, the jockey does not sit in the saddle, he crouches over it, leaning all his weight on his toes, which rest on the thin metal bases of stirrups dangling about a foot from the horse's topline. When a horse is in full stride, the only parts of the jockey that are in continuous contact with the animal are the insides of the feet and ankles—everything else is balanced in mid-air. In other words, jockeys squat on the pitching backs of their mounts, a task much like perching on the grille of a car while it speeds down a twisting, potholed freeway in traffic. The stance is, in the words of University of North Carolina researchers, "a situation of dynamic imbalance and ballistic opportunity." The center of balance is so narrow that if jockeys shift only slightly rearward, they will flip right off the back. If they tip more than a few inches forward, a fall is almost inevitable. A Thoroughbred's neck, while broad from top to bottom, is surprisingly narrow in width, it offers little for the jockey to grab to avoid plunging to the ground and under the horse's hooves. (pp. 70–71)

I love that passage. I have never been particularly interested in horse racing, but that passage, so beautifully written, demands my interest. It makes me pay attention. To use Lamott's term, it "unfolds" that world in a way that fascinates me. It draws me in.

If great passages draw us in, they will draw our students in as well. In searching for passages to share with our students, maybe we should start by looking for intriguing writing that captures worlds most familiar to them. What student, for example, wouldn't be interested in this passage from Eric Schlosser's *Fast Food Nation: The Dark Side of the American Meal*?

> The McDonald's Corporation has become a powerful symbol of America's service economy, which is now responsible for 90 percent of the country's new jobs. In 1968, McDonald's operated about one thousand restaurants. Today it has about thirty thousand restaurants worldwide and opens almost two thousand new ones each year. An estimated one out of every eight workers in the United States has at some point been employed by McDonald's. The company annually hires about one million people, more than any other American organization, public or private. McDonald's is the nation's largest purchaser of beef, pork, and potatoes—and the second largest purchaser of chicken. The McDonald's Corporation is the largest owner of retail property in the world. Indeed, the company earns the majority of its profits not from selling food but from collecting rent. McDonald's spends more money on advertising and marketing than any other brand. McDonald's operates more playgrounds than any other private entity in the United States. It is one of the nation's largest distributors of toys. A survey of American schoolchildren found that 96 percent could identify Ronald McDonald. The only fictional character with a higher degree of recognition was Santa Claus. The Golden Arches are now more widely recognized than the Christian cross. (p. 4)

While just about everyone has pursued a hamburger at McDonald's, how many people have had the hamburger pursue them? Alfred Lansing's great nonfiction work *Endurance: Shackleton's Incredible Voyage* recounts the harrowing struggle for survival by British explorer Ernest Shackleton and his twenty-five men as they were trapped in the Arctic ice for sixteen months. Facing starvation, one of the men, storekeeper Thomas Orde-Lees, ventures across the ice on a hunting expedition. Unsuccessful, hungry, and tired, he is heading back to camp when suddenly a strange, hungry beast springs out of nowhere and tries to devour him:

> Traveling on skis across the rotting surface of the ice, [Orde-Lees] had just about reached camp when an evil, knoblike head burst out of the water just in front of him. He turned and fled, pushing as hard as he could with his ski poles and shouts for Wild [the second-in-command] to bring his rifle.
>   The animal—a sea leopard—sprang out of the water and came after him, bounding across the ice with the peculiar rocking-horse gait of a seal on land. The beast looked like a small dinosaur, with a long, serpentine neck.
>   After a half-dozen leaps, the sea leopard had almost caught up with Orde-Lees when it unaccountably wheeled and plunged into the water. By then, Orde-Lees had nearly reached the other side of the floe; he was about to cross safe ice when the leopard's head exploded out of the water directly

in front of him. The animal had tracked his shadow across the ice. It made a savage lunge for Orde-Lees with its mouth open, revealing an enormous array of sawlike teeth. Orde-Lees' shouts for help rose to screams and he turned and raced away from his attacker. The animal leaped out of the water again just as Wild reached his rifle . . . (p. 102)

When we read great passages, whether about horses, hamburgers, or hungry beasts, we feel a need to share them—celebrate them—with our adolescent readers. In a way, we, avid readers ourselves, are pearl divers, swimming through oceans of text, looking for gems to share with students. We want our students to see the intellectual rewards we uncover and to appreciate how beautiful reading can be. After sharing a number of great passages with my students, I ask them to uncover their own pearls to share with the class. (This, by the way, is a great strategy to end classroom reading time—go around the room and have everyone read the single most provocative line they have come across during the period. Or give students a strip of cash register tape and have them write down their favorite line with a marker and hang them in the room. Or have a bulletin board entitled "I Didn't Know That!" and have students write and illustrate something they learned that day by reading.)

Though there are eight other major reasons to read, the idea that reading brings pleasure and knowledge remains first and foremost in my mind. I hope to make it first and foremost in the minds of my students as well.

Reason 2: Reading Builds a Mature Vocabulary

Let's say that tomorrow you take an extended sabbatical from teaching. You decide to leave the classroom to pursue your lifelong dream of sailing around the world. In addition to sailing around the globe, you make up your mind to build your own boat before setting sail, and you decide that you are the one who will do the actual sailing. Incidentally, you know nothing about sailing or boat building, but you are resolved that with intense work and determination, you will be able to set sail within a couple of months.

To begin building your boat, you rent a large truck and drive off to the nearest Home Depot. You're not exactly sure what materials you'll need, so you purchase anything you think will be useful. After loading up the rental truck, you drive home, dump the materials in your backyard, say good-bye to your significant other (who by now has packed and is leaving), and start building. Without any help, and with a great deal of trial and error, your boat takes shape. Three months pass, and after many more trips to the hardware store, you believe your boat, patchwork as it is, to be seaworthy.

You haul your boat to the shore. Before launching, you ask gathered friends and family if they'd like to join you on your around-the-world adventure. You reassure them that even though your knowledge of sailing is limited, you've studied hard in the past two months, and, as skipper of the vessel, you promise to try your hardest. It's now time to set sail. Who wants to go?

My guess is that you'll be sailing alone. Why? Because you did not take the many long-term steps necessary to become a qualified boat builder and sailor. A serious sailor would have to learn how to shape wood and fiberglass, how to furl a sail, read a sextant, operate a ham radio, ration food. No matter how intense the desire, one cannot just wake up one morning and instantaneously become a sailor, let alone a boat builder. It takes years before one would be ready to set sail on the high seas.

Likewise, a nonreading high school senior cannot wake up one morning three months before graduation and decide to acquire a mature vocabulary for college or the workplace. Students who have been slackers for a number of years can't suddenly decide to prepare for college midway through the senior year. Like the sailor building a boat, a student needs to take many steps to develop a mature vocabulary. Students must be taught the value of vocabulary acquisition long before they graduate, and engaging in daily independent reading is a necessary step to building vocabulary. There is no magic vocabulary "pill."

How many nonreaders have you met who scored resoundingly high on the verbal section of the SAT? None? But I have yet to meet a voracious reader who did not possess a mature vocabulary.

Reason 3: Reading Makes You a Better Writer

In *The Power of Reading,* Stephen Krashen makes the point that the research "strongly implies that we learn to write by reading. To be more precise, we acquire writing style, the special language of writing, by reading." Krashen, citing numerous studies, notes "that children who participate in free reading programs write better, and those who report they read more write better" (pp. 72–73).

One study conducted by the National Assessment of Educational Progress (NAEP) at the fourth- and eighth-grade levels underscored the flip side of this reading-writing connection. As part of this study, the teachers of 6,692 fourth graders and 7,651 eighth graders were asked about their instructional and assessment techniques. Among the major findings, "a significant relationship between having students provide written responses and higher reading scores was observed" (p. 1). Students given more multiple-choice exams scored lower on reading assessments than students who were frequently assigned written exams. In short, students who *wrote* more ended up *reading* better.

Carol Booth Olson, in *The Reading/Writing Connection,* notes that "reading and writing have been thought of and taught as opposites—with reading regarded as receptive and writing as productive." But researchers have found, Olson notes, that reading and writing are "essentially similar processes of meaning construction" and that readers and writers "share a surprising number of characteristics" (p. 17):

- Both readers and writers actively engage in constructing meaning from and with texts.
- Both move back in order to go forward in a recursive process.
- They interact and negotiate with both reading and writing—that is, they keep writing in mind when reading and reading in mind when writing.
- They use a common tool kit of cognitive strategies—planning and setting goals, tapping prior knowledge, asking questions, making connections, summarizing, monitoring, revising meaning, reflecting, and evaluating.
- They use skills automatically.
- They are self-motivated and confident.

Olson nicely captures what we, as teachers, know intuitively: that reading improves one's writing, and that writing improves one's reading. Almost without exception, our students who are excellent writers are also those who do the most reading, and those who are the best readers are often the best writers.

Ron and Jan Strahl, directors of the South Basin Writing Project at Long Beach State University, encapsulate this idea when they tell teachers in training, "We must write like readers and read like writers." When we read, we need to metacognitively be aware of the skill, the strategies, the techniques used by the author. When we write, we must always consider audience and purpose, always keeping our reader in mind.

In short, reading and writing cannot be viewed as separate activities—each helps the other. We know this. Our students need to know this, too.

Reason 4: Reading Is Hard, and "Hard" Is Necessary

In the movie *A League of Their Own,* Geena Davis plays Dottie Hisson, a member of a women's professional baseball team formed while World War II is being waged. Dottie is the star player of the team, which is managed by Jimmy Dugan, played by Tom Hanks. Late in the movie, Dottie decides she has had enough of baseball, the hardships of travel, and the pressures of playing. Even though she loves baseball, it has all become, in her words, "too hard." She shocks Jimmy with the news that she is quitting. Dugan can't believe what he's hearing:

> **Jimmy Dugan:** Quitting? You'll regret it for the rest of your life! Baseball is what gets inside you. It lights you up. You can't deny that.
> **Dottie Hisson:** It just got too hard!
> **Jimmy Dugan:** It's supposed to be hard! If it wasn't hard, everyone would do it. The "hard" is what makes it great.

Being a great baseball player is meaningful because *becoming* a great baseball player requires hard work. Think of an accomplishment in your life of which you are deeply proud. Chances are there's a lot of hard work behind that accomplishment. Rarely does half-hearted effort produce deep pride. While it's true that not everyone can become a star baseball player, we must believe that all our students, given the right motivation, teaching, and reading materials, can make meaning from hard text.

We all have students in our classes who give up easily when faced with difficult reading. Often these students will read a difficult passage one time, find it "too hard," and look to the teacher for the answer. In some classrooms students have almost been trained *not* to do the hard work. Karen Feathers, in her book *Infotext,* coined the phrase "reader's welfare" for teachers who provide answers without their students doing the work. We must keep our students from learning helplessness by emphasizing the necessity and beauty of hard work.

Sheridan Blau, former president of the National Council of Teachers of English and currently a professor at the University of California, Santa Barbara, stresses that students must be taught to embrace confusion. Confusion is necessary, he argues, before real learning can occur. If you are reading something unchallenging, you might be entertained, but you limit what you learn. Rather than shutting down and giving up when reading becomes confusing, students need to learn that comprehension of difficult text does not occur instantaneously. Rather, comprehension develops incrementally. Difficult reading is necessary to make rich meaning. We must teach students that it's all right not to understand something the first time they read it. It's the "hard" that makes comprehending difficult reading great. "Hard" is necessary. "Hard" is a good four-letter word.

While we're on the subject of hard text, I have a confession to make: even though I have read *Hamlet* over fifty times and have taught it twelve years to approximately forty classes and over 1,400 students, I still don't completely understand the play. Every time I read it I see something new in it. After all these years I am still struggling to understand *Hamlet.* It's the "hard" that makes *Hamlet* great. Yet, ridiculously, we hand a play like *Hamlet* to seventeen-year-old reluctant readers and expect them to read it one time and "get it."

Unfortunately, teachers have become expert at hiding their struggles with difficult reading material. Consider what you do the night before you plan on bringing something challenging into the classroom for students to read. When planning a scene in *Hamlet,* for example, I do some serious preparation at home. I reread the scene and often highlight and write comments on my copy of the play. I also revisit some of the critical analysis I have gathered over the years to strengthen my background knowledge. Then I might reread the scene again. If, after all this preparation, I'm still feeling a little insecure, I'll pop in a CD and listen to the scene in my car on my way to school.

My students think I'm smarter than I am because I come to class as someone who really "knows" this difficult play. They don't know that when I read *Hamlet* the first time it was as difficult for me as it is for them. When I walk into the classroom, all they see is an "expert." They don't see the hours of intense preparation I undertook to deepen my understanding of the play. They don't see the struggle I had with the "hard." I have hidden that struggle from them.

While my students struggled with the hard parts, I was frequently guilty of exacerbating their difficulty by adopting what I call a "Gotcha!" mentality. My Gotcha! mentality went something like this: I assigned students to read Chapter 3 for homework. When the students arrived in class the next day, I wanted to find out who "got" the reading and who didn't. To measure their level of comprehension, or whether they read the chapter at all, I would spring a reading check on them, usually in the form of a pop quiz. If I gave them three questions, one might be concerned with literal recall, but the others would be attempts to measure whether they understand the "hard" parts of the chapter. Though my intentions were good—I wanted to assess where kids were struggling with the text—I admit I sometimes took a secret perverse pleasure in writing questions, some real zingers, I knew might catch them. Gotcha!

I have come to recognize the Gotcha! approach as counterproductive to the idea of getting students to develop a willingness to read difficult material. I now believe the same homework assignment should go something like this: "Take Chapter 3 home tonight to read. Please identify the parts of the chapter that give you the most comprehension problems. Identify the hard parts by either highlighting the troublesome passages, writing your questions on a blank bookmark, or marking them with post-it notes. Tomorrow we will begin class in small groups, and I will expect everyone to share at least one thing you do not understand. Be prepared to bring your confusion to the group tomorrow to discuss and work through. Confusion is necessary to deepening our understanding, and it should be uncovered and embraced. Expect to be confused, but be prepared to discuss what good readers do when they become confused."

In helping students to understand the necessity of reading difficult text, we must share with them that we have all found a rich reading experience in something we did not "get" at first. We must prepare students to recognize that there will always be difficult text in their future and that the skills involved in reading difficult material continuously develop through life.

Furthermore, reading difficult text allows us to grow what I call "prior knowledge Velcro," so that future difficult reading has something to stick to. People who have a wide range of prior knowledge are more likely to comprehend difficult text because they are more likely to be able to make connections to that reading. They are able to activate the appropriate schema, the appropriate background information, to make comprehension possible. If you know absolutely nothing about a topic, it is next to impossible to comprehend a difficult reading selection on that topic. The more background knowledge you have, the more schema you possess, and the more connections you can make, the easier it will be to read and make sense of the text. Experienced readers are more likely able to possess and activate the appropriate schema when engaged with new and unfamiliar text.

It also helps to remember that all of us are good readers and that all of us are also bad readers—it depends on what we're reading. I have seen a lot of "poor" readers in my classes become much better readers when given a skateboard magazine or comic book. Conversely, I have seen a lot of "good" adult readers become awful readers when asked to read a tax form or investment newsletter. (Here's an interesting homework assignment: tell the students to bring reading material to class that they think you, the teacher, will have trouble reading. You might be confronted with directions for advancing in a video game or instructions on how to rip and burn a new CD off the Internet. Show them your struggle as you read what they bring you. Model how you cope with the problem, and have the students take notes of the reading strategies you employ to make sense of the passage.) Students must see that we are all good readers and bad readers, and that we continue learning to read the hard stuff throughout our lives. Developing as a reader never stops, and learning to read hard material is an integral part of that development.

One last thought about reading hard text: I have stopped expecting my students to like everything I ask them to read. As teachers, we hope all our students will love every great work of literature as much as we do. In actuality, this is unrealistic. Every year, for example, I know some of my seniors will not like reading George Orwell's *1984*. (The confusion in *1984* begins with its first sentence: "It was a bright cold day in April, and the clocks were striking thirteen.") Though *1984* is my favorite book to teach, I know some students will not be as enamored with it as I am. Nevertheless, I expect all my students to see the *value* of reading *1984*. After reading the novel, I expect they will think about the world they will soon inherit in a different light. Whether they like *1984* or not, reading it will give them new insight into government, politics, privacy issues, and notions of individuality. There is value in the struggle to read this book, whether you like the book or not. There is a difference between *liking* a book and *valuing* a book. If I teach well, maybe my students will do both.

Reason 5: Reading Makes You Smarter

During her junior year, Jennifer Schymick, a biochemistry major at MIT, wrote the passage below while working on the Human Genome Project. Please read it and see if you can answer the two questions that follow.

Using Bioinformatics to Finish Draft Sequence of Human Chromosome 16
A primary goal of the Human Genome Project (HGP) is to determine the complete sequence of the three billion DNA bases comprising the human genome. Although we have declared 90–95% draft coverage for the genome, most of the current draft sequence remains fragmented and unorganized. In order to achieve the goal of complete coverage for human chromosome 16 (chr16), we have implemented numerous bioinformatic tools and resources to order and orient sequences contigs, close gaps, and ensure correct overlap between clone projects consisting primarily of draft sequence. The chr16

project has incorporated sequence generated by LANL and the PGF, as well as, sequence provided by other centers. By using BAC and other sequences from the TGR database, we have created a tilting set of minimal overlapping BAC clones to efficiently optimize sequence coverage. From this minimal tilting set, we have identified regions of overlap between projects and, consequently, have incorporated or "stolen" data from one project into another. Stealing has had numerous advantages by increasing sequence depth, cloning contig gaps, and providing information to order and orient contigs within each clone project. Stealing also allows us to directly compare sequence between potentially overlapping clones, to ensure correct overlap, and to help detect regions of large sequence duplications within the chromosome. We are currently using information from ordered BAC clone sequences to complete the minimum tilting set and provide overall ordered sequence coverage for chr16. Ultimately, on the way to achieving finished data, all ordered and oriented clones are submitted to Genbank as Phase 2 submissions.

1. True or False: Reading this passage is harder than counting dimpled chads.
2. True or False: Jennifer, the author of the above passage, is one bright young woman who read voraciously as a child.

The answer to the first question is a tough call. The second question, of course, is rhetorical; we can tell from the piece of writing that Jennifer has read a great deal in her life. Though it's true Jennifer has worked very hard to get to MIT, it's also true she is fortunate. Her mother is an English and reading teacher who is an expert in children's and adolescent literature. Jennifer was virtually born with a book in her hands. (This reminds me of one of my favorite tabloid headlines: "Baby Born Singing Christmas Carols." In Jennifer's case the headline would read, "Baby Born Reading.") Voluminous reading was a given in Jennifer's life.

Jennifer's upbringing underscores the importance that reading plays in developing intelligence. Terrence Paul, in *Patterns of Reading Practice*, notes that "the quantity of books available is the best single predictor of test score performance and success in schools, and is a better predictor than socioeconomic status or parental education. This is directly related to 'literacy-rich environments in which reading is reinforced as a pleasurable and important activity'" (p. 4). In other words, student success starts with access to good books. Show me a child of any race, from any socioeconomic background, surrounded by great books and enthusiastic people to model the benefits of reading, and I'll show you a budding lifelong reader. Access to good reading makes one a reader, and being a reader makes one smarter. How many students at MIT do you think were read to as youngsters? How many students at MIT do you think are reluctant readers?

There is growing evidence that suggests that reading not only makes you smart, it *keeps* you smart as you age. Among recent studies are the following:

- A landmark study released in 2000 by the Alzheimer's Association examined pairs of elderly twins in which one of the twins had dementia while the other one had remained healthy. The researchers found that low education was a significant risk factor for Alzheimer's disease and all other forms of dementia. Further analysis showed that twins who later became demented read fewer books, particularly as adults, compared to their nondemented siblings.

- Reading habits between the ages of six and eighteen appear to be crucial predictors of cognitive function decades later, according to Dr. David Bennett of Chicago's Rush University. Bennett believes the brain should be challenged early to build up more "cognitive reserve" to counter brain-damaging disease later in life. This view is shared by Dr. Margaret Gatz, professor of psychology at UCLA, who notes that "cognitive reserve—greater levels which may be marked by educational achievement—may act as a cushion against intellectual impairment" (Neergaard 2001).

- Researchers used to believe that our brain stopped growing after age five. "Scientists now know the brain continually rewires and adapts itself, even in old age," notes Lauran Neergaard, medical writer for the Associated Press. "Large brain-cell growth continues into the teen years; and even the elderly can grow at least some new neurons . . . Scientists say it's never too late to jog the gray matter."

- Dr. Amir Soas, a co-investigator of a groundbreaking study on the effects of aging on the brain, notes that his research also points to a "use it or lose it" conclusion. Soas advises baby boomers who want to lower their chances of Alzheimer's to stay mentally engaged. "Do crossword puzzles," he advises. "Pull out the chessboard or Scrabble. Learn a foreign language or a new hobby." Soas strongly suggests you turn the television off, because when you watch it, "your brain goes into neutral." Soas also recommends three critical steps everyone should do to keep their minds sharp as they age: "Read, read, read."

As noted in the *Reading/Language Arts Framework for California Public Schools* all this recent research "indicates that the volume of reading affects general cognitive development" (p. 186). In layman's terms, the more you read, the smarter you'll become, and the smarter you become, the more likely you'll remain sharp in your golden years. Consider reading as a rustproofing treatment of the brain.

Reason 6: Reading Prepares You for the World of Work

In *Teaching the New Basic Skills: Principles for Educating Children to Thrive in a Changing Economy*, Richard Murnane and Frank Levy visited a number of large corporations around the country to get an idea of what employers are looking for in new employees. They then visited a number of schools, from elementary-level to high school, to determine whether students were being taught these necessary skills to succeed in the new economy. Their findings are sobering. Murnane, a professor at the Harvard Graduate School of Education, and Levy, a professor of Urban Economics at MIT, found the following:

- There is an "increasingly dramatic disparity between the skills children are currently acquiring within our education system and the skills they will need to obtain good jobs in an increasingly, globally influenced job market" (p. xiv).
- "As recently as the 1950s, twenty percent of the jobs in America were professional, twenty percent skilled, and sixty percent unskilled. In the 1990s, twenty percent of the jobs remained professional, but skilled jobs rose to sixty-plus percent while unskilled jobs fell below twenty percent" (p. vii).
- "The skills required to earn a decent income have changed radically, but what is taught in most of our schools has changed little, if at all . . . The educational system is undergoing *incremental* improvement in an environment of *exponential* change. This fact implies that the educational improvement at the present rate will result in fewer and fewer young people being prepared for a global economy" (p. xv).
- "The gap between the average annual earnings of high school and college graduates has widened significantly in the past fifteen years" (p. ix).
- "No longer will today's high school diploma lead to a job that will guarantee entry into the middle class" (p. vii).

In coming to the conclusion that students are leaving high school without the skills necessary to compete, Murnane and Levy argue that we must do a better job of teaching both "hard" and "soft" skills. The "hard" skills include basic mathematics, problem solving, and reading abilities at levels much higher than many high school graduates now attain. The "soft" skills include the ability to work in groups and to make effective oral and written presentations.

I must confess I have always been a bit skeptical of the school-to-work movement. As a teacher, I do not want to reduce my job to being an in-house trainer for IBM or Microsoft. After all, shouldn't they train their own employees? But I've come to realize it really isn't about IBM or Microsoft at all. It's about making my students strong readers, proficient writers, and critical thinkers. In helping them develop in these ways, I am giving my students options—options for them to be able to work wherever they choose. Conversely, if I fail to teach them, I am limiting their possibilities. As Murnane and Levy point out, "In this world you go to war every day, and short of becoming a millionaire, a very good education is your best armor" (p. 4). Reading well is the core of this armor.

Reason 7: Reading Well Is Financially Rewarding

I like to remind my students occasionally that they are being paid to attend my class today—not just in cognitive stimulation and intellectual enlightenment, but in cold, hard cash. Consider the following (based on a forty-year career, using 2000 U.S. Census figures):

- The average lifetime earnings for a student who does not finish high school is $936,000.
- The average lifetime earnings for a student who does finish high school is $1,216,000.
- Therefore, a high school diploma is worth $280,000 ($1,216,000 minus $936,000).
- Four years of high school (assuming some time off for illness) amounts to 700 days of school.
- Therefore, students are "paid" $280,000 for 700 days of school.
- Therefore, students earn $400 per day.
- Therefore, students earn $66.67 to attend my class each day (based on a six-period day). Students who finish college will earn a lot more per day than that.

Of course, whenever I tell my students this, I'm usually asked something like, "Where's my money?" I then remind them that plumbers, doctors, and car mechanics do not get paid until the job is finished. Thus far, I have been lucky: no student has remembered to hit me up on graduation night.

After graduation, students will need more money than they think. To gauge their immediate post–high school costs, have students fill out the form on the following page. Keep in mind that this planning guide addresses only short-term, post–high school plans. After renting an apartment, students are likely one day to want a home of their own. It's not too early to consider these long-term costs. What is the average down payment for a home in their area? How much money will they need to qualify for a home loan? How much are mortgage payments, as opposed to rent payments, likely to be?

And that's just housing. What about other long-term expenses? Ask your students how many would like to get married? have children? vacation in Maui? own a big-screen TV? purchase furniture? pay landscaping costs? afford home, car, and life insurance? have medical and dental coverage for their spouse and children? Life is much more expensive than adolescents realize. (According to an article in the June 13, 2001, issue of the *Kansas City Star,* the average cost of raising one child is $165,630—about $233,530 after inflation. Having two children who are generously supporting our local orthodontist, I tend to think these figures are on the conservative side.)

After considering all these expenses, ask your students the key questions: What will your annual income have to be to maintain your desired lifestyle after high school? What will your income need to be ten, twenty, thirty years

Calculating Monthly Cost of Living

Part 1 | Cost

FOOD AND HOUSING (you might want a roommate to help share costs):

Rent: Find the cost of a 1–2-bedroom apartment by looking in the newspapers. | _____

Phone/Utilities/Cable: This varies with the season, apartment size, appliances. $200 a month is average. Remember that long distance calls can cost more, depending on your plan. | _____

Food: Check supermarket ads to figure your food budget. Remember to include lunches at work as well as soap, toothpaste, pet food, etc. Food can range from $200 to $500. | _____

TRANSPORTATION: You'll have lots of choices and price ranges—bicycle, bus, car pool, new or used car (remember maintenance, insurance, and repairs). The cost can range from $300 to $450. | _____

CLOTHING: This depends on your style, talents, and climate. Do you sew? look for sales? splurge? Remember shoes, underwear, and coats. Start with $100 plus a month. | _____

ENTERTAINMENT: You're probably familiar with the price of movies and concerts. Remember to include books, magazines, CDs. Allow at least $100. | _____

OTHER ITEMS: Higher-cost items include health care, dental care, and life insurance. Lower-cost items include such things as cosmetics, gifts, haircuts, laundry. | _____

EDUCATION: Will you be going to college or a trade school? What are the costs of tuition, books, parking, fees? | _____

SAVINGS: Invest in your future. How much will you save? | _____

Total Cost of Part 1 | _____

Part 2
TAXES: To estimate approximate federal, state, social security, and other taxes, add up the monthly amounts you listed in Part 1 and multiply that figure by 30% (.30). For example, if your total monthly cost is $1,000, your total cost for taxes would be an additional $300.

Total Cost of Part 2 | _____

Part 3
Add Part 1 and Part 2 to find out how much you will need to earn each month.

Total Monthly Cost | $ _____

(Source: San Mateo County Office of Education)

from now? How are you going to earn enough money to support the lifestyles you desire? What is the connection between developing your reading skills now and preparing for your economic future? How will reading well support you in your quest to live your desired lifestyle?

When discussing their financial goals, it is important for students to realize that the demands of the workforce are radically changing. According to the 2000 U.S. Census, in 1975 a worker with a bachelor's degree made 1.5 times more than a worker with a high school diploma. By 1999, however, that gap had widened, with the college graduate earning 1.8 times more than the high school graduate. Similarly, workers with advanced degrees earned 1.8 times more than high school graduates in 1975; that gap had grown to 2.6 times the high school graduate's earnings in 1999. Clearly, the demand for skilled workers has increased, and every indication is that this demand will continue to increase. Poor readers will be left behind.

I'm guessing that your students are like mine: they need help in seeing the importance that reading has in their future financial lives. They need to learn that their academic behavior today plays a major part in determining their economic future.

Reason 8: Reading Opens the Door to College and Beyond

We have all heard that our schools are failing, that they are not serving the needs of our students. While this may be true in some specific places, particularly in our inner cities, overall I don't buy it. The competition for admission to our best universities, despite increasingly stringent entrance requirements, is more intense than ever. This year at UCLA, for example, 10,522 students were admitted, but the real story is who *didn't* get in—7,755 applicants who had graduated from high school *with a 4.0 or higher grade point average.* Nearly eight thousand straight-A students denied admission! The average SAT verbal score for a student admitted to UCLA was 642. The average math SAT score was 678. The competition for college admission is fierce, both at UCLA and nationwide, which suggests that for those students who are serious about their education, public schools are doing a better job of preparing them than ever before.

There are a number of factors admission officers consider when reviewing a student's application, among them:

* the number of advanced placement (AP) classes taken by the applicant
* the applicant's SAT and SAT II scores
* the student's personal essay

Each of these criteria underscores the importance of being able to read well. Let's look at the reading demands of each of these admission requirements.

Advanced Placement Courses

High school students taking an AP literature course in hopes of becoming eligible for admission to the university of their choice will be tested on their ability to comprehend difficult text. Here, for example, is an actual AP passage in English language and composition found on a recent exam:

> Vast and primeval, unfathomable, unconquerable, bastion of cottonmouth, rattlesnake and leech, mother of vegetation, father of mosquito, soul of the silt, the Okefenokee is the swamp archetypal, the swamp of legend, of racial memory, of Hollywood. It gives birth to two rivers, the St. Mary's and the Suwannee, fanning out over 430,000 leaf-choked acres, every last one as sodden as a sponge. Four hundred and thirty acres of stinging, biting and boring insects, of maiden cane and gum and cypress, of palmetto, slash pine and peat, of muck, mud, slime, and ooze. Things fester here, things cook down, decompose, deliquesce. The swamp is home to two hundred and twenty-five species of birds, forty-three of mammals, fifty-eight of reptiles, thirty-two of amphibians and thirty-four of fish—all variously equipped with beaks, talons, claws, teeth, stingers, and fangs—not to mention the seething galaxies of gnats and deerflies and no-see-ums, the ticks, mites, hookworms, and paramecia that exist only to compound the misery of life. There are alligators here, bears, puma, bobcats, and bowfin, there are cooters and snappers, opossum, coon, and gar. They feed on one another, in the sludge and muck and on the floating mats of peat they bury their eggs, they scratch and stink and sniff at themselves, caterwauling and screeching through every minute of every day and night till the place reverberates like some hellish zoo. (Source: The College Board)

After reading this passage students are asked to write an essay in which they analyze how the distinctive style of the passage reveals the purpose of its writer. Not an easy task, even for the brightest of our students. An impossible task if you lack higher-level reading skills.

SAT I and II

It doesn't get any easier on the SATs. The following is an actual passage used on a recent exam (from *Real SAT II*, 1998). Read it and consider the questions that follow the passage:

> I have one word to say upon the subject of
> profound writers, who are grown very numerous
> of late; and I know very well, the judicious
> world is resolved to list me in that number. I
> conceive therefore, as to the business of being
> profound, that it is with writers as with wells—

a person with good eyes may see to the bottom of
the deepest, provided any water be there; and
that often, when there is nothing in the world at
the bottom, besides dryness and dirt, though it
be but a yard and a half under ground, it shall
pass, however, for wondrous deep, upon no
wiser a reason than because it is wondrous dark.

I am now trying an experiment very frequent
among modern authors; which is to write upon
Nothing; when the subject is utterly exhausted,
to let the pen still move on; by some called the
ghost of wit; delighting with walking after the
death of its body. And to say the truth, there
seems to be no part of knowledge in fewer hands,
than that of discerning when to have done. By the
time that an author has writ out a book, he and
his readers are become old acquaintances, and
grow very loth to part; so that I have sometimes
known it to be in writing, as in visiting, where
the ceremony of taking leave has employed more
time than the whole conversation before. (1704)

Which of the following is the most appropriate interpretation of the figurative language in lines 6–8 ("it is . . . be there")?

A. If the writing is truly profound, it is beyond ordinary human understanding.
B. If the writing has any substance, it can be understood by an intelligent reader.
C. The true meaning of a work is whatever an intelligent reader wants it to be.
D. If writing is to be truly profound, the ideas must be conveyed in a complicated style.
E. A complicated style of writing is often a disguise for a shallow intelligence.

Given the terms of comparison in lines 6–13, "dryness and dirt" (line 10) can be best interpreted as

A. inflexible beliefs
B. conventional attitudes
C. pornographic fancies
D. barren thoughts
E. down-to-earth realities

A new SAT will be administered for the first time in March 2005. According to the College Board, the upcoming changes that are being made include the following:

- The former SAT Verbal Exam will become the SAT Critical Reading Exam. This test will no longer include analogies. Instead, short reading sections will be added to the present long reading passages.
- A new section called the SAT Writing Exam will be added. This section will contain multiple-choice grammar questions as well as a written essay.

When you consider the actual reading passage shown previously and the fact that the new test will add even more passages, it is easy to conclude that high school students have little chance of performing well on the SAT unless they are very capable readers. Though students may boost their score by taking a preparation course, they will not be able to read critically at this level without having had a number of years of prolific reading and writing.

The Personal Essay

Personal essays are designed to measure college applicants' writing abilities; and, as argued earlier, reading ability goes a long way toward making a good writer. When reading my students' essays, I can easily discern which of them are readers. It is evident in their choice of diction, their sentence structure, their rhythm, their voice, their craft. If these traits are evident to us, their high school teachers, they are equally evident to college admission readers. Outside of plagiarism, college-level writing can't be faked.

Other factors, such as community service and evidence of leadership, are used in making college admission decisions, but these are moot if the applicant cannot read well. These three factors (AP, SAT, and the personal essay) are gates students must pass through to gain admission to college. These gates can only be opened with the key of reading. This key is cut through years of voracious reading.

If reading opens the door to college, it also keeps the door from shutting on the students once they are admitted. The amount of reading required at the college level is often a shock to freshmen, particularly for those who did not do much reading in high school. I'll never forget the Contemporary Literature class I took my junior year. I had to read fifteen novels in fifteen weeks. I clearly remember having to take a night off from my work as an executive table technician (sounds better than a waiter, doesn't it?) in order to catch up on my reading. I had a plan that night: to read the last 200 pages of *Sophie's Choice* and then read the first 100 pages of *Lolita*. Only in college would such a strange juxtaposition occur! I had to read at a furious pace to survive this class; but this reading was for only one of my classes. I was taking three other courses, each of which had serious reading demands. Had I not entered college as a reader, I surely would have drowned.

Reading well in junior and senior high school not only allows students to gain admittance to college, it also goes a long way in making sure they leave with a diploma in hand.

Reason 9: Reading Arms You Against Oppression

There is a growing body of evidence suggesting that "school readiness" as early as kindergarten plays a significant role in children developing into readers. The U.S. Department of Education conducted a longitudinal study of kindergartners in the class of 1998–1999 in which they assessed kindergartners' performance on a number of reading tasks. Among the statistically significant findings were the following:

- Asian and white children were more likely than children in other racial/ethnic groups to be proficient across all reading tasks. In some areas of reading, the differences were substantial, exceeding one-half of a standard deviation.
- Socioeconomic status (SES) was related to proficiency across all reading tasks. Children in higher SES groups were more likely to be proficient than children in lower SES groups.
- Parents in higher SES groups were more likely to read every day to their children than were parents of the lower SES groups. The difference was substantial.

It's not much of a stretch to see that students who enter kindergarten with a low level of school readiness are at risk of falling behind their peers in subsequent years. Incredibly, I was once told by a consultant in the California Department of Education that the governor's office looks at fourth-grade reading scores to determine how much money the state needs to allocate for building future prison space. The thinking goes that if fourth-grade reading scores are low, we can expect more prisoners ten years from now and that we should start building additional prisons in anticipation of that need. In other words, students in elementary school who can't read very well have a much greater chance of being incarcerated later in their lives.

It's scary to contemplate that a child's academic future may be largely dictated by socioeconomic background. Although there certainly are exceptions, the fourth grader who is significantly behind grade level in reading will most likely still be behind grade level in the sixth grade, the ninth grade, and the twelfth grade. Unfortunately, many junior high students who fall in this category are not given enough extra time, enough high-interest reading material, and enough motivation to read. Sadly, these students, who need acceleration, are often placed in remedial classes where the pace is slowed. Needing more, they are given less—ensuring that they will never catch up. As a result, many students are graduating from high school with weak reading skills, thus maximizing their chances of future economic hardship and oppression.

Though we know that family income and parental education play a large part in our students' academic success, we cannot accept these facts as insurmountable hurdles. As Kati Haycock, Director of the Education Trust, notes, recent research has shown that "what schools do matters enormously. And what matters most is good teaching." Haycock cites the following:

- A 1998 Boston study of the effect public school teachers have on learning: "In just one academic year, the top third of teachers produced as much as six times the learning growth as the bottom third of teachers. In fact, 10th graders taught by the least effective teachers made nearly no gains in reading and even lost ground in math."
- "Groundbreaking research in Tennessee and Texas shows that these effects are cumulative and hold up regardless of race, class, or prior achievement levels. Some of the classrooms showing the greatest gains are filled with low-income students, some with well-to-do students . . . It's not the kids after all: Something very different is going on with the teaching" (p. 28).

In short, teaching matters a great deal. When students are put in the care of experienced, qualified, motivated teachers, they do well. When my high school students enter my classroom unmotivated and below grade level in reading, I must remind myself that first and foremost, my duty in the next 180 days—my mission, if you will—is to change their perceptions about reading. As a high school teacher, I may be their last chance to develop a level of proficiency that will enable them to fend for themselves, to avoid the oppression that often afflicts the uninformed in our society.

Am I exaggerating? Think of a time in your life when your inability to read something accurately cost you. Maybe you didn't read the fine print on a traffic ticket or on a car loan. Perhaps you read a contract incorrectly or were charged a late fee because you misread a bill. Possibly you misunderstood a crucial essay question or were denied voting privileges because you missed the registration date. Maybe you bounced a check because you did not read your checkbook correctly. All of us have been taken advantage of at one point or another because of our failure to read something accurately. And yet all of us are college graduates; all of us are good readers. If this happens to us, what will happen to those who leave our schools unable, or unwilling, to read?

The ability to read will become increasingly important in the near future. The amount of information available to human beings doubles every six months, and in the last 400 weeks of human existence 500 million computers worldwide have been plugged in. We are in the infancy of an information age, and weak readers will be left behind.

James Baldwin was right when he said, "It is expensive to be poor." Beyond simple economics, Baldwin was getting at the notion that poor people are often taken advantage of. The best way to arm our students against this oppression is to teach them how to read the world critically—to teach them how to read the advertiser who is trying to get them to spend their money unwisely; to read the politician who is intentionally clouding the issue; to read the ballot proposition correctly. If we teach them these things, it will be much harder for someone to take advantage of them.

Reading Reasons Across the Content Areas

This book is not just for language-arts teachers. All teachers, regardless of subject area, have an obligation to teach both their subject matter *and* to develop their students' literacy. Beyond literature and poetry, high school graduates today are expected to read nonfiction, magazines, journals, newspapers, primary source documents, charts, maps, graphs, applications, warranties, contracts, speeches, essays, editorials, policy statements, manuals, consumer and workplace documents, ballots, and Internet information. Do we really want to place this entire reading burden on the backs of English teachers?

example

There is hope out there. Last week I visited a remarkable history classroom. The teacher had decorated every wall and the entire ceiling with covers of *Time* magazine (literally hundreds of them). There was a classroom library front and center in the room, stocked with books and magazines, not all on history. SSR time was honored and treated with respect. The message emanating from that history classroom was loud and clear: reading is important. It would not take a student entering that classroom more than ten seconds to understand the value that history teacher places on reading.

Teachers are campaign managers

But it takes more than a beautifully decorated room to move students to read. It takes a coordinated plan. In a way, getting students to become readers is much like getting a politician elected to office. Both tasks require serious, well-coordinated campaigns. If, as campaign manager, I wanted to convince people to vote for my candidate, I would be foolish to put all my resources and energies into only one precinct. What sort of campaign would target only one neighborhood? Imagine seeking only one important endorsement! Would an effective campaign run all its television and radio commercials on one station only? How effective would a campaign be if it pitched its audience during a set time of day and never varied from that timing?

Regardless of how appealing my candidate might be, using these narrow approaches would minimalize the chances of being elected. Likewise, in a campaign to motivate kids to read it would be foolish for students to hear all the reasons to read from only one teacher, during only one period in the school day. Motivating readers is not a content-specific job and should not be left to one teacher. The campaign to motivate adolescents to read must reach across the content areas, across the school day, across the school year. We all share in the responsibility of developing our students' literacy. When teachers across the curriculum unite to sell reading, our students stand a much better chance of internalizing the message. With this in mind, the mini-lessons in the next chapter are not content-area specific—any teacher of any subject in any classroom can use them. We all want students to lead lives in which reading matters.

No Pig Kissing!

Every year there seems to be an article in the newspaper on how a school has reached its predetermined reading goal. The piece is usually accompanied by a photograph of the principal rewarding the students by doing something silly—kissing a pig, shaving his beard, or sleeping on the school roof. The students in the background of these photographs always seem to be enjoying the spectacle immensely. But I wonder whether it will take an even more outlandish stunt for the following year's classes to reach their reading goals. Are we sending the wrong message to our students by performing stunts to get them to read?

Instead of offering students extrinsic reasons to read, we should be teaching students why reading will benefit them. In the next chapter you will find forty mini-lessons, one for every week of the school year, each answering the question "Why should I read?" Each mini-lesson falls under one of the nine reading reasons introduced in this chapter. Each takes between five and twenty minutes to teach and can be used in any content-area classroom as soon as tomorrow morning.

More important, the goal of each of these mini-lessons is to help your students develop meaningful, intrinsic reasons to read. They are meant to make the reasons we love to read visible to our students. You will not find suggestions of free pizza or pig kissing in these pages. What you will find are forty answers to share with students who are wondering, "What's in it for me?"

3

THE FORTY MINI-LESSONS

In this chapter you will find forty mini-lessons, one for each week of the school year. These mini-lessons address the nine reading reasons outlined in Chapter 2:

1. Reading is rewarding.
2. Reading builds a mature vocabulary.
3. Reading makes you a better writer.
4. Reading is hard, and "hard" is necessary.
5. Reading makes you smarter.
6. Reading prepares you for the world of work.
7. Reading well is financially rewarding.
8. Reading opens the door to college and beyond.
9. Reading arms you against oppression.

Although they are grouped around each of the nine reading reasons, the mini-lessons can be taught randomly (in fact, that is how I prefer to present them). They are numbered here just to make them easy to locate. Each mini-lesson in this chapter takes between five and twenty minutes to teach, which is convenient if you ever finish a lesson a few minutes short.

It's also a good idea for students to have a specific place to organize and reflect upon these reading reasons. My students have used marble-colored, hundred-page composition books for this purpose. These books are bound, have a sturdy cardboard cover, and are relatively inexpensive. Post-it notes may be used as dividers to separate the book into nine sections, one for each reading reason. For each mini-lesson, students may either copy the lessons or use glue sticks to affix the quotations, graphs, and charts on the left-hand side of their open books. They can then use the right-hand pages on which to write their reflections. The books are stored in the classroom for easy access and serve as constant reminders why reading is important.

Reading Is Rewarding

Favorite First Lines

Reading
Builds a
Mature
Vocabulary

Reading
Makes You a
Better Writer

Reading Is
Hard, and
"Hard" Is
Necessary

Reading
Makes You
Smarter

Reading
Prepares You
for the World
of Work

Reading Well
Is Financially
Rewarding

Reading
Opens the
Door to
College and
Beyond

Reading Arms
You Against
Oppression

Never judge a book by its cover—and, I might add, never judge a book by its first few pages. Nevertheless, when opening a new book it has been a habit of mine to take note of the first line. I know when I write that sometimes the first line is the hardest, so I like to see how authors choose to begin their works, how they draw their readers in. It's fun to get students to keep track of their favorite first lines. This activity helps students appreciate good writing. When we ask students to take notice of excellent writing, we give them the message that writing is a craft and should be appreciated. Students who learn to appreciate the craft of good writing learn that reading for reading's sake is fun.

1. Ask your students, "How many of you sometimes have a hard time deciding how to start an essay?" Point out that this often happens to the best of writers.

2. Explain to students that even though we should not judge an entire book by its first couple of pages, it's interesting to take note of how authors choose to begin their books.

3. Share with students some interesting first lines from your favorite books.

4. As the school year progresses, have students keep track in their notebooks of their favorite first lines. First lines do not necessarily have to be the first words of a book—they can be expanded to include the first words of a chapter, the first words of a newspaper or magazine article, the first words of a poem, etc.

5. At least once a year construct a classroom bulletin board entitled "Favorite First Words." Give each student an index card or strip of blank cash register tape and have him or her write a favorite line. Make a favorite first line collage.

Reading Reasons: Motivational Mini-Lessons for Middle and High School. Kelly Gallagher. Copyright © 2003. Stenhouse Publishers.

Favorite First Lines from Books

"The old lady had changed her mind about dying but by then it was too late." *City of Bones*, Michael Connelly

"If you are interested in stories with happy endings, you would be better off reading some other book." *The Bad Beginning*, Lemony Snicket

"On a night even demons howl for their mothers, Josh stood on the edge of the highway, thumbing a ride." *Sang Spell*, Phyllis Reynolds Naylor

"Here's something I can do without: people standing in front of me in the supermarket line who are paying for an inexpensive item by credit card or personal check. People! Take my word for this: Tic Tacs is not a major purchase." *Brain Droppings*, George Carlin

"For three weeks, the killer actually lived *inside the walls* of an extraordinary fifteen-room beach house." *Kiss the Girls*, James Patterson

"Deep in the past during a spectacular cruel raid upon an isolated Ojibwa village mistaken for hostile during the scare over the starving Sioux, a dog bearing upon its back a frame-board tikinagun enclosing a child in moss, velvet, embroideries of beads, was frightened into the vast carcass of the world west of the Otter Tail River." *The Antelope Wife*, Louise Erdrich

"The man in the dog suit whines outside the door." *Flying Leap*, Judith Budnitz

"They shoot the white girl first." *Paradise*, Toni Morison

"Nick Taylor had been called many things since becoming chief spokesman for the Academy of Tobacco Studies, but until now no one had actually compared him to Satan." *Thank You for Smoking*, Christopher Buckley

"I have been afraid of putting air in a tire ever since I saw a tractor tire blow up and throw Newt Hardbine's father over the top of the Standard Oil sign." *The Bean Trees*, Barbara Kingsolver

"Novalee Nation, seventeen, seven months pregnant, thirty-seven pounds overweight—and superstitious about sevens—shifted uncomfortably in the seat of the old Plymouth and ran her hands down the curve of her belly." *Where the Heart Is*, Billie Letts

"On a cold, blowy February day a woman is boarding the 10 A.M. flight to London, followed by an invisible dog." *Foreign Affairs*, Alison Lurie

Reading Reasons: Motivational Mini-Lessons for Middle and High School. Kelly Gallagher. Copyright © 2003. Stenhouse Publishers.

The Reading Minute

Reading
Builds a
Mature
Vocabulary

Reading
Makes You a
Better Writer

Reading Is
Hard, and
"Hard" Is
Necessary

Reading
Makes You
Smarter

Reading
Prepares You
for the World
of Work

Reading Well
Is Financially
Rewarding

Reading
Opens the
Door to
College and
Beyond

Reading Arms
You Against
Oppression

At the beginning of each class period, a piece of interesting reading is shared with the class. This sharing usually takes a minute or less, and there are no follow-up assignments. The shared reading can come from a range of sources, from poetry to nonfiction. The selections may be culled from newspapers, magazines, novels, textbooks—anywhere we, as readers, come across interesting text. All the Reading Minutes share one goal: to demonstrate to our students that there is a world of reading richness out there.

1. For the first month of school, I conduct the Reading Minute. I pick an interesting passage or article to read to the students. Often I pick something from the current book I am reading, or I cut something out of the morning newspaper or current magazine to share (there is always at least one high-interest article in the daily newspaper—if we read the paper from a student's point of view).

2. After I read my selection, students open their notebooks to their "Reading Minute" section. On a sheet of notebook paper, I have them write the day's date and a one-sentence summary or thesis statement to remember today's Reading Minute. (This also helps to make sure they all pay attention during the Reading Minute.) I am strict about one sentence only—this also helps develop their summary skills.

3. In October, students begin leading the Reading Minute. For sign-ups, I print a calendar for the remainder of the school year. Each student in each period must sign up for five days between October and June. On the days they sign up, they are responsible for the Reading Minute. I encourage them to spread out their sign-up days to give them the opportunity to read a range of materials. Thus, each student will conduct five different Reading Minutes between October and June. If any open days remain, I conduct the Reading Minute those days.

4. When a student finishes sharing, the class is required to say, "Thank you."

5. At the end of the school year, students should have 150–180 summary sentences of all the interesting reading that was shared. This reinforces that reading in itself is a rich and rewarding pursuit. As an end-of-the-year reflective assignment, students can write about the Reading Minutes. Possible topics:

• Which Reading Minute was your favorite?
• Which Reading Minute taught you something?
• Is there value in the Reading Minute assignment?
• Should I require next year's students to continue the Reading Minute?

Reading Reasons: Motivational Mini-Lessons for Middle and High School. Kelly Gallagher. Copyright © 2003. Stenhouse Publishers.

Ideas for Sharing During the Reading Minute

What kinds of passages should you share?

Passages you find beautiful

Passages you find interesting

Passages that exhibit great writing

Passages that anger you

Passages that trouble you

Passages that perplex you

Passages that raise your curiosity

Passages you find humorous

Passages that challenge you to think differently

Where should you find passages?

Books (fiction and nonfiction)

Poetry

Newspapers

Magazines

Speeches

Essays

Internet material

Maps

Graphs

Charts

Manuals

MINI-LESSON

2

Reading Wisdom

Reading
Builds a
Mature
Vocabulary

Reading
Makes You a
Better Writer

Reading Is
Hard, and
"Hard" Is
Necessary

Reading
Makes You
Smarter

Reading
Prepares You
for the World
of Work

Reading Well
Is Financially
Rewarding

Reading
Opens the
Door to
College and
Beyond

Reading Arms
You Against
Oppression

We want students to see that for people from all walks of life, the rewards of reading are profound. While it's good for students to hear this message in their teachers' words, the wisdom collected for this mini-lesson enables me to make this reminder forty different times in ways far more eloquent than I alone could express.

1. Have a space in your room labeled "Reading Thought of the Week." Post a different thought weekly and have the students copy them.

2. Have students reflect and respond to the quotations. In the left-hand column, students copy the reading wisdom passage. In the right-hand column, they share their thoughts about the passage. They can agree, disagree, argue, question, challenge, or make connections to other ideas or passages. These reflections can be done each week or at the end of each month, quarter, or semester.

Reading wisdom	My response

3. At the end of the quarter or semester, have students choose the one quote most meaningful to them and have them share in one or all of the following ways:

    - Give an oral report on your favorite passage.
    - Write an essay reflecting on the meaning of your favorite passage and its relevance to you.
    - Share in small groups, and then nominate one quote from each group to be shared with the entire class.
    - Include the selections as part of the students' end-of-year portfolio.

4. Challenge students to find reading wisdom quotes on their own and bring them to class to share.

Reading Reasons: Motivational Mini-Lessons for Middle and High School. Kelly Gallagher. Copyright © 2003. Stenhouse Publishers.

Reading Wisdom

The illiterate of the future is not who cannot read or write, but one who cannot learn, unlearn, and relearn. *Alvin Toffler*

To read without reflecting is like eating without digesting. *Edmund Burke*

In times of change, learners inherit the earth, while the learned find themselves beautifully equipped to deal with a world that no longer exists. *Eric Hoffer*

A person who doesn't read is no better off than a person who can't read. *Mark Twain*

'Tis the good reader that makes the good book. *Ralph Waldo Emerson*

Literature is no one's private ground, literature is common ground; let us trespass freely and fearlessly and find our way for ourselves. *Virginia Woolf*

A good reader is one who has imagination, memory, a dictionary, and some artistic sense. *Vladimir Nabokov*

A book must be an ice ax to break the frozen sea within us. *Franz Kafka*

The reading of all great books is like conversation with the finest men of past centuries. *René Descartes*

A man is known by the company his mind keeps. *Thomas Bailey Aldrich*

We don't always choose the books we read . . . sometimes they choose us. *Rubin "Hurricane" Carter*

I read my way out of poverty long before I worked myself out of poverty. *Walter Anderson*

The only things worth reading are things you don't understand. *Sheridan Blau*

Anonymous Quotes

Books impede the persistence of stupidity. *Spanish proverb*

Nothing can stop a person who wants to be educated. Nothing can help a person who doesn't.

When you finish reading a book you are a more interesting person.

All great books are challenging and should be challenged.

What's worse than burning books? Not reading them.

Reading does not teach you how to read. It teaches you how to read better.

We read to know we are not alone.

The book that can be read without any trouble was probably written without any trouble also.

In any one book there is more than any one reader can see.

WARNING: reading may lead to an increase in knowledge, altered perceptions, and deepened insight. All such reactions are normal, but may lead to a serious reading habit.

Good readers have a greater tolerance for failure.

Reading Reasons: Motivational Mini-Lessons for Middle and High School. Kelly Gallagher. Copyright © 2003. Stenhouse Publishers.

Who Lives in Your House?

Reading
Builds a
Mature
Vocabulary

Reading
Makes You a
Better Writer

Reading Is
Hard, and
"Hard" Is
Necessary

Reading
Makes You
Smarter

Reading
Prepares You
for the World
of Work

Reading Well
Is Financially
Rewarding

Reading
Opens the
Door to
College and
Beyond

Reading Arms
You Against
Oppression

There is an old Spanish proverb, "Show me who your friends are and I'll tell you who you are." I like to adapt that to read, "Show me the books you have in your home and I'll tell you who you are." Because many of our students may not have any books in their homes, we need to model for them that educated people develop personal libraries. We surround ourselves with great minds and take comfort knowing they "live" with us.

1. Share a list of ten noted authors who "live" in your house. I like mixing contemporary and classical writers to model to students a wide range of interesting minds. With students in small groups, ask them how many of the people they can identify.

2. Share answers as a class. Have each group fill in any possible blanks by having a classroom sharing session.

3. Once all of the people are identified, ask the students what these ten people have in common. Have students discuss in small groups and then share possible responses to the class.

4. Once the student responses are heard, share your answer: all ten of these people "live" in my house. Read a sample preselected passage from some of them. Share the beauty and wisdom of these authors with your students. Here, for example, is a passage from Carl Sagan's *Cosmos*:

> *The Earth is a place. It is by no means the only place. It is not even a typical place. No planet or star or galaxy can be typical, because the Cosmos are mostly empty. The only typical place is within the vast, cold, universal vacuum, the everlasting night of intergalactic space, a space so strange and desolate that, by comparison, planets and stars and galaxies seem achingly rare and lovely. If we were randomly inserted into the Cosmos, the chance that we would find ourselves on or near a planet would be less than one in a billion million trillion (10^{33}, a one followed by 33 zeroes). In everyday life such odds are compelling. Worlds are precious.*

Carl Sagan lives in my house. Explain to students the comfort you receive by being surrounded by statesmen, writers, athletes, artists, and scientists—in short, greatness.

5. Have students brainstorm a list of ten famous people they would like to have live at their house. Chances are there is a great book about each person they list.

Answer key: **Lincoln**—president during Civil War; **Jordan**—considered by many to be the greatest basketball player ever; **Shakespeare**—considered by many to be the greatest English author; **Seinfeld**—comedian; **Morrison**—Nobel-prize–winning author; **Marquez**—Nobel-prize–winning author; **Murray**—Pulitzer-prize–winning sportswriter; **Jefferson**—founding father; **Sagan**—astronomer; **Poe**—author.

Reading Reasons: Motivational Mini-Lessons for Middle and High School. Kelly Gallagher. Copyright © 2003. Stenhouse Publishers.

How many of the following ten people can you identify?

Person	Why is this person famous?
Abraham Lincoln	
Michael Jordan	
William Shakespeare	
Jerry Seinfeld	
Toni Morrison	
Gabriel Garcia Marquez	
Jim Murray	
Thomas Jefferson	
Carl Sagan	
Edgar Allan Poe	

What do these ten people have in common?

MINI-LESSON

4

Reading Builds a Mature Vocabulary

Brain Food

Reading
Builds a
Mature
Vocabulary

Reading
Makes You a
Better Writer

Reading Is
Hard, and
"Hard" Is
Necessary

Reading
Makes You
Smarter

Reading
Prepares You
for the World
of Work

Reading Well
Is Financially
Rewarding

Reading
Opens the
Door to
College and
Beyond

Reading Arms
You Against
Oppression

Developing a vocabulary is largely achieved through repeated exposure to unfamiliar words in context. In short, it's a numbers game. The more you read, the more new words you encounter. The more new words you encounter, the more new words you learn. It's not a coincidence that students who read the most are usually the students with the broadest vocabularies—vocabularies they began building in infancy by listening to those around them and developed through reading a wide range of genres.

1. Ask students why it's important to read unfamiliar words.

2. Share and discuss the first two key points on the next page: (1) research demonstrates that preschoolers with large vocabularies tend to become proficient readers; and (2) we develop mature vocabularies by being exposed to unusual words in context.

3. If you have already worked through the "Don't Be Such a Borf!" mini-lesson (page 56), revisit it. Remind students that by reading one sentence they learned an unfamiliar word. Reiterate the importance of reading unfamiliar, or "rare," words.

4. Reveal the Number of Rare Words Met per Thousand charts (both listening and reading). Ask students to complete the left-hand side of this chart:

What do these charts mean?	My reflections on these charts

5. Share possible meanings in groups. Clarify.

6. Have students reflect in the right-hand column. What kind of materials are they reading? What kind of materials should they be reading?

Reading Reasons: Motivational Mini-Lessons for Middle and High School. Kelly Gallagher. Copyright © 2003. Stenhouse Publishers.

We develop mature vocabularies by being exposed to unusual words in context. With this in mind, let's look at a study that measured the amount of unusual words we come across from various listening and reading sources.

Number of Rare Words Met per Thousand

Listening

	Rare words per thousand
Adult to child, 6 months	9.3
Adult to child, 3 years	9.0
Adult to child, 10 years	11.7
Adult to adult	17.3
Prime time TV	22.7

Reading

	Rare words per thousand
Children's book	30.9
Adult book	52.7
Comic book	53.5
Popular magazine	65.7
Newspaper	68.3
Scientific paper	128

(*Source:* Hayes and Ahrens 1988)

MINI-LESSON

5

Building Your Vocabulary

Reading Is
Rewarding

Reading
Builds a
Mature
Vocabulary

Reading
Makes You a
Better Writer

Reading Is
Hard, and
"Hard" Is
Necessary

Reading
Makes You
Smarter

Reading
Prepares You
for the World
of Work

Reading Well
Is Financially
Rewarding

Reading
Opens the
Door to
College and
Beyond

Reading Arms
You Against
Oppression

Reading words in context is critical to vocabulary development. Sometimes the context is so strong that we learn the word on an initial reading. Other times we learn words incrementally—that is, we understand shades or partial meanings until we have seen the word in context enough times to finally arrive at a full understanding. Though teachers must still teach vocabulary directly, students must see that most vocabulary acquisition comes through reading multiple genres and authors.

1. Ask students, "Is it important to develop the ability to read unfamiliar words?" Have them list specific examples later in life where the ability to read unfamiliar words might become important (examples: a contract or job application).

2. Present the four unfamiliar vocabulary words in this mini-lesson (gloaming, gloriole, glossitis, and gloxinia) to the students and ask them to predict the meaning of each word, without any context.

3. Ask students what strategies they employed to try to guess the correct definitions (e.g., look at prefixes, suffixes, and roots; compare with sound-alike words).

4. Allow students to read each of the vocabulary words in the context sentence.

5. Have students revise their guesses after reading the words in sentences.

6. Reveal the actual definitions (see below).

7. Ask students how many words they were able to guess partial or full meaning of based on the context.

8. Ask students to consider what will happen to their vocabularies if they read a lot.

Definitions
gloaming: (n) the period of fading light after sunset but before dark.
gloriole: (n) a halo around somebody's head.
glossitis: (n) inflammation of the tongue.
gloxinia: (n) a popular house plant with large, colorful, bell-shaped flowers.

Reading Reasons: Motivational Mini-Lessons for Middle and High School. Kelly Gallagher. Copyright © 2003. Stenhouse Publishers.

Predict the meaning of the following words:

Word	Guess without context	Revised guess after context
Gloaming		
Gloriole		
Glossitis		
Gloxinia		

Context

1. Even though it's not completely dark, you should turn the headlights of your car on during the *gloaming*.

2. The angel had a *gloriole* above her head.

3. With a swollen tongue like that, he must have *glossitis*.

4. Imelda planted three *gloxinias* in a big pot in her apartment.

Reading Is
Rewarding

Reading
Builds a
Mature
Vocabulary

Reading
Makes You a
Better Writer

Reading Is
Hard, and
"Hard" Is
Necessary

Reading
Makes You
Smarter

Reading
Prepares You
for the World
of Work

Reading Well
Is Financially
Rewarding

Reading
Opens the
Door to
College and
Beyond

Reading Arms
You Against
Oppression

Don't Be Such a Borf!

Unfortunately, many students skip unfamiliar words without even attempting to decipher their meaning. In doing so, they are missing out on valuable chances to improve their vocabulary. We must demonstrate to them that good readers use context while reading, and that doing so helps them to develop mature vocabularies. The best "bang for the buck" in acquiring vocabulary comes from regular reading, but only if we embrace unfamiliar words by examining the context around them.

1. Ask students why it's important to develop a mature vocabulary. List answers on board (examples: having a mature vocabulary might help in a job interview, raise SAT scores, or assist them to read more difficult material).

2. Give students the "gliff" sentence and ask them to predict its meaning.

3. Explain to students that they have never seen the word "gliff" before (you know this to be true because it is a made-up nonsense word). Ask students how they were able to decipher the correct answer even though they had never seen the word "gliff" before.

4. Have students create their own nonsense words (with definitions). Have each student write a sentence with a nonsense word in it, providing enough context for the reader to figure it out. Have students exchange and guess the meanings of their nonsense words (or collect student papers, pull out the ten best examples, and give them a mock vocabulary quiz the following day).

5. Discuss the notion that even expert readers come across unfamiliar words. When they do so, they don't simply ignore the word; they use sentence context clues in an attempt to make some meaning from the word in question.

6. Distribute newspapers to the students. Have each student find three words he or she is unfamiliar with. Have the student copy each unfamiliar word in its complete sentence. Underline the unfamiliar words and write definition predictions. Check your prediction with other students in small groups. Consult dictionaries to see if your predictions are accurate.

7. Emphasize that students will not learn any "gliffs" unless they read a lot. By reading regularly, students expose themselves to unfamiliar vocabulary in meaningful context and, in doing so, build mature vocabularies. Reading is what builds a strong vocabulary—there are no shortcuts. Revisit the benefits of having a mature vocabulary (step 1).

Reading Reasons: Motivational Mini-Lessons for Middle and High School. Kelly Gallagher. Copyright © 2003. Stenhouse Publishers.

Read the sentence in the box and predict the meaning of the underlined word:

It was so <u>gliff</u> outside, I had to wear two sweaters and a jacket!

"Gliff" most likely means:

(A)   warm.

(B)   cold.

(C)   bright.

(D)   dark.

Reading Reasons: Motivational Mini-Lessons for Middle and High School. Kelly Gallagher. Copyright © 2003. Stenhouse Publishers.

Word Attack!

Reading
Makes You a
Better Writer

Reading Is
Hard, and
"Hard" Is
Necessary

Reading
Makes You
Smarter

Reading
Prepares You
for the World
of Work

Reading Well
Is Financially
Rewarding

Reading
Opens the
Door to
College and
Beyond

Reading Arms
You Against
Oppression

Students are often at a loss of what to do when they encounter an unfamiliar word. Ask a student what strategy he or she employed when confronted with a new word, and often the response will be, "I didn't do anything. I kept reading." One strategy we can model for students is to demonstrate how good readers break down new words—to mine for word parts (prefixes, roots, suffixes) that might suggest at least a partial meaning. Rather than avoiding unfamiliar words, this lesson teaches students to be aggressive, rather than passive, readers when confronted with unfamiliar vocabulary.

1. Put the word *pneumonoultramicroscopicsilicovolcanoconiosis* on the board or overhead. Tell the students this is an actual word in the dictionary and have them try to figure out in small groups at least a partial meaning by breaking the word down.

2. After students struggle with the word a bit, reveal the sentence that shows them the word in the context of a sentence. Have them continue to work at trying to define the word.

3. Ask students which parts of the word they were able to break down and generate meaning from. String these on the board or overhead until the students figure out the definition of the word or until they have hit a dead end.

4. If necessary, reveal the definitions of the word parts.

5. If necessary, reveal the definition of the entire word.

6. Ask students the following:

   • Who would probably be more capable of breaking down a word like this—someone who reads rarely or someone who reads frequently?
   • Why? Explain.

7. Have students share their responses until they come to the idea that regular reading increases our chances of making meaning from unfamiliar vocabulary and that good readers employ word-attack strategies when faced with unfamiliar vocabulary.

Reading Reasons: Motivational Mini-Lessons for Middle and High School. Kelly Gallagher. Copyright © 2003. Stenhouse Publishers.

Define this word:

pneumonoultramicroscopicsilicovolcanoconiosis

Context sentence

Because of his closeness to Mount St. Helens, he contracted *pneumonoultramicroscopicsilicovolcanoconiosis.*

Word roots

pneumono: related to the lungs

ultra: super

micro: small

scopic: related to a viewing instrument

silico: the mineral silicon

volcano: eruption in the earth from which molten rock, steam, and dust issue

coni (konis): dust

osis: referring to a diseased condition

Definition

Pneumonoultramicroscopicsilicovolcanoconiosis is a disease of the lungs caused by habitual inhalation of very fine silicon dust particles.

(*Source:* Readence, Bean, and Baldwin 2000)

MINI-LESSON
8

Reading Makes You a Better Writer

Reading Is
Rewarding

Reading
Builds a
Mature
Vocabulary

Reading
Makes You a
Better Writer

Reading Is
Hard, and
"Hard" Is
Necessary

Reading
Makes You
Smarter

Reading
Prepares You
for the World
of Work

Reading Well
Is Financially
Rewarding

Reading
Opens the
Door to
College and
Beyond

Reading Arms
You Against
Oppression

Cooking Up Good Writing

If you aspired to be an excellent artist, you would no doubt familiarize yourself with as many artists and their styles as possible. You might visit as many museums and galleries as possible. You would study the history of art, the media used, the various styles and techniques. In short, to advance your own artistic abilities, you would immerse yourself in great art. This emersion would give you the proper background to assist you in finding your own style. If this holds true for emerging artists, then it might be reasonable to assume that the same principles apply to emerging writers as well. After all, writing is art, too. To develop writers, we need to flood them with examples of great writing.

1. If you have already done the mini-lesson "Reading as a Writing Model" (page 64), revisit it to review the reasons why it's important to develop writing abilities.

2. Share the How to Become a Good Chef list with the class.

3. Share the How to Become a Good Musician list with the class.

4. Share the blank How to Become a Good Writer list with the class. With the other examples in mind, have students fill in the missing items. Their answers might look like this:

How to Become a Good Writer
- Read lots of books.
- Understand the ingredients of good writing.
- Play with the ingredients of good writing.
- Sample lots of writers.
- Imitate other writers.
- Experiment with different combinations of writing.
- Learn from your failures.
- Practice, practice, practice.

5. Have students write a reflection on how to become a good writer. How does prolific reading help you develop as a writer?

Reading Reasons: Motivational Mini-Lessons for Middle and High School. Kelly Gallagher. Copyright © 2003. Stenhouse Publishers.

How to Become a Good Chef

- Read a lot of recipes.

- Understand the ingredients of good cooking.

- Play with the ingredients of good food.

- Sample lots of chefs.

- Imitate other chefs.

- Experiment with different combinations of food.

- Learn from your failures.

- Practice, practice, practice.

How to Become a Good Musician

- Read a lot of music.

- Understand the ingredients of good music.

- Play with the ingredients of good music.

- Sample lots of musicians.

- Imitate other musicians.

- Experiment with different combinations of music.

- Learn from your failures.

- Practice, practice, practice.

How to Become a Good Writer

-
-
-
-
-
-
-

Reading Reasons: Motivational Mini-Lessons for Middle and High School. Kelly Gallagher. Copyright © 2003. Stenhouse Publishers.

MINI-LESSON

9

Reading Is
Rewarding

Reading
Builds a
Mature
Vocabulary

Reading Is
Hard, and
"Hard" Is
Necessary

Reading
Makes You
Smarter

Reading
Prepares You
for the World
of Work

Reading Well
Is Financially
Rewarding

Reading
Opens the
Door to
College and
Beyond

Reading Arms
You Against
Oppression

Reading as a Writing Model

Many reluctant readers are also reluctant writers. When they do compose, their writing lacks rhythm and development. Their paragraphs often look something like this: six words, then a period. Five words, period. Six words, period. Seven words, period. Five words, period. End of paragraph. No use of dependent clauses. No compound or complex sentences. No sentence branching. No vivid description. Having done minimal reading and writing in their lives, they have not seen enough models to internalize what good writers do.

Even if our students do not grow up to be English teachers, we want them to understand the importance of developing their writing skills. Students must see that strong writing is a powerful tool, and reading provides a way to hone that tool.

1. Have the class brainstorm a list of why it's important to develop writing skills. List examples where the ability to write produced results (examples: a job application, a letter of complaint to a merchant, a letter of concern to a senator, a strong editorial).

2. Show students Writing Sample 1, an abridged passage from John Steinbeck's *Of Mice and Men.* (It might help to explain that a bunkhouse is kind of like a dorm room for cowboys.) Ask them to evaluate the effectiveness of the description of the bunkhouse. Ask them to consider the strengths and weaknesses of the paragraph. (Possible strength: some description; possible weaknesses: underdeveloped, all simple sentences.)

3. Have students read Writing Sample 2, Steinbeck's actual passage. Ask them which of the two passages is better.

4. Questions for discussion:

   - Why is the second passage better writing than the first? (Possible answers: much better description, more sentence variety/rhythm.)
   - How do we develop more rhythm in our writing? (By reading and writing frequently.)
   - How does reading help us develop our writing? (Reading provides writing models. If we read enough, these models become internalized and we acquire the ability to write with more rhythm.)

If time permits . . .
Have the students describe your classroom by modeling the Steinbeck passage sentence by sentence. Example: The classroom was a small, square room. Inside, the walls were brick painted white and the floors were gray tile. On three walls were student projects, from colored maps of Europe to . . .
Or
For homework, have students find examples of what they think is great writing. Have students bring the examples to class and explain why these passages are great.

Reading Reasons: Motivational Mini-Lessons for Middle and High School. Kelly Gallagher. Copyright © 2003. Stenhouse Publishers.

Writing Sample 1

The bunkhouse was a long building. Inside it was plain. It had three doors and small windows. There were eight bunks. Some of the bunks had blankets. Some had burlap ticking. Each bunk had shelves. Each shelf had the cowboy's belongings. There was also medicine and other stuff on the shelves. Near one wall was a stove. In the middle of the room was a table to play games on.

Writing Sample 2

The bunkhouse was a long, rectangular building. Inside, the walls were whitewashed and the floor unpainted. In three walls there were small, square windows, and in the fourth, a solid door with a wooden latch. Against the walls were eight bunks, five of them made up of blankets and the other three showing their burlap ticking. Over each bunk there was nailed an apple box with the opening forward so that it made two shelves for the personal belongings of the occupant of the bunk. And these shelves were loaded with little articles, soap and talcum powder, razors, and those Western magazines ranch men love to read and scoff at and secretly believe. And there were medicines on the shelves, and little vials, combs; and from nails on the box sides, a few neckties. Near one wall there was a black cast iron stove, its stovepipe going straight up through the ceiling. In the middle of the room stood a big square table littered with playing cards, and around it were grouped boxes for the players to sit on.

(*Source: Of Mice and Men* by John Steinbeck)

Reading Is
Rewarding

Reading
Builds a
Mature
Vocabulary

Reading
Makes You a
Better Writer

Reading Is
Hard, and
"Hard" Is
Necessary

Reading
Makes You
Smarter

Reading
Prepares You
for the World
of Work

Reading Well
Is Financially
Rewarding

Reading
Opens the
Door to
College and
Beyond

Reading Arms
You Against
Oppression

Says Who?

After they read Chapter 1 of *Lord of the Flies,* I asked students to revisit the chapter again and write down all the words William Golding used as synonyms for "said." Here is the list:

went on	asked	explained	whispered
shrieked	persisted	muttered	insisted
shouted	cried	exclaimed	answered
spoke	mentioned		

When we read, good writing is modeled for us. Seeing these models over a period of time makes us better writers.

1. Have students predict the meaning of the following three words: *taunt, attest,* and *wail.*

2. After making their predictions, reveal the following sentences to the students:

    "Your dress is the ugliest one at the dance," *taunted* Allison.
    "There's the killer!" the witness *attested* as she pointed to the defendant.
    "Give me back my toy!" the two-year-old *wailed.*

3. After reading the words in context, allow students to revise their predictions.

4. Ask students what these three words have in common (answer: they are all synonyms for *said*).

5. Have students brainstorm as many words as they know that could serve as synonyms for *said.* Chart them.

6. Share the Synonyms for "Said" sheet with students.

7. Ask students to reflect on the following questions:

    • Why not just use the word *said* only?
    • Why do authors use different words for *said*?
    • How do we, as young writers, learn variations of words like *said*?
    • How do we, as young writers, learn variations of other words that will strengthen our writing?
    • Why is it important to develop broader vocabularies?
    • How does reading help us to become better writers?

Reading Reasons: Motivational Mini-Lessons for Middle and High School. Kelly Gallagher. Copyright © 2003. Stenhouse Publishers.

Synonyms for "Said"

acknowledged	demurred	maintained	responded
acquiesced	denied	mentioned	restated
added	denounced	mimicked	resumed
addressed	described	moaned	retorted
admitted	dictated	mumbled	returned
admonished	directed	murmured	revealed
advised	disclosed	mused	roared
advocated	disrupted	muttered	ruled
affirmed	divulged	nagged	sanctioned
agreed	drawled	narrated	scoffed
alleged	droned	noted	scolded
allowed	elaborated	notified	screamed
announced	emphasized	objected	shouted
answered	enjoined	observed	shrieked
approved	entreated	opined	snapped
argued	enunciated	orated	sneered
asked	estimated	ordered	sobbed
assented	exclaimed	petitioned	solicited
asserted	exposed	pled	spoke
assumed	expressed	pointed out	sputtered
attested	faltered	prayed	stammered
avowed	feared	predicted	stated
babbled	foretold	proclaimed	stipulated
bantered	fumed	professed	stormed
bargained	giggled	prompted	stressed
began	grinned	propounded	suggested
boasted	grunted	publicized	taunted
called	held	quibbled	thought
claimed	implied	ranted	threatened
commented	indicated	reassured	told
complained	inferred	reciprocated	twitted
confided	instructed	refuted	urged
contradicted	itemized	related	uttered
cried	laughed	remonstrated	vowed
debated	lectured	repeated	wailed
decided	lied	replied	warned

MINI-LESSON
11

Slim Shadings

Reading Is
Rewarding

Reading
Builds a
Mature
Vocabulary

Reading
Makes You a
Better Writer

Reading Is
Hard, and
"Hard" Is
Necessary

Reading
Makes You
Smarter

Reading
Prepares You
for the World
of Work

Reading Well
Is Financially
Rewarding

Reading
Opens the
Door to
College and
Beyond

Reading Arms
You Against
Oppression

If you want to know who the real readers in your class are, have them write an essay. Voracious readers exhibit the same signs when they write: complex sentence structure, use of strong verbs, and evidence of a mature, nuanced vocabulary. (Reading broadens a student's vocabulary. A broadened vocabulary makes the student a better writer.) Whenever I see these signs, more often than not I have a reader in my midst. Voracious reading creates word shadings in our students' vocabularies.

1. Brainstorm a list with students all the words a writer might use instead of the word "very."

2. Share with them the list of synonyms for "very." Ask the students why we have so many different words that mean "very." Why not just have a single word ("very") and leave it at that?

3. Ask students to consider the following words: *slim, skinny,* and *slender.* Have them answer the following questions:

   • Is there a difference between *slim, skinny,* and *slender?* Which of these words has the most positive connotation? The most negative connotation?
   • As writers, why is it important to have different shadings of words?
   • How does reading help to develop these shadings? (Consider the "very" synonyms.)

Reading Reasons: Motivational Mini-Lessons for Middle and High School. Kelly Gallagher. Copyright © 2003. Stenhouse Publishers.

Look at some of the possibilities writers use instead of using the word "very":

intensely	exceedingly	bitterly	surely
especially	unusually	truly	richly
mightily	powerfully	infinitely	severely
chiefly	shockingly	immeasurably	slightly
incredibly	fully		

Why do you think there are so many synonyms for "very"? Why not just have the single word "very"?

Now, consider these three words:

slim

slender

skinny

MINI-LESSON

12

Reading Is Hard, and "Hard" Is Necessary

Reading Is
Rewarding

Reading
Builds a
Mature
Vocabulary

Reading
Makes You a
Better Writer

**Reading Is
Hard, and
"Hard" Is
Necessary**

Reading
Makes You
Smarter

Reading
Prepares You
for the World
of Work

Reading Well
Is Financially
Rewarding

Reading
Opens the
Door to
College and
Beyond

Reading Arms
You Against
Oppression

Driving Good Reading

Isn't it amazing how the most reluctant adolescent reader will suddenly become Evelyn Woods when it comes to reading the *Department of Motor Vehicles Handbook*? This phenomenon usually occurs somewhere around age fifteen. The DMV handbook is a nice example of how we must sometimes buckle down to read informational text, and of how careful readers reap clear benefits.

1. Individually, ask students to take the nine-question driving handbook quiz.

2. In addition to taking the exam, have students make a list of strategies they employed to read and answer the questions correctly.

3. Have students share their answers in small groups and then as a whole class.

4. Brainstorm a list of reading strategies that good readers employ when faced with an exam like this one. Your students might generate some of the following answers:

    *   I eliminated obvious wrong answers.
    *   I highlighted key words.
    *   I narrowed my choices down to two possible answers and guessed.
    *   I remember my father getting a ticket for this.
    *   I reread the question two, three, four, or more times.
    *   I thought back to when I read that specific rule in the *Driver's Handbook*.
    *   I skipped problems and came back. (I answered the easy ones first.)

5. Brainstorm: What other kinds of exams will you take in your lives where these reading strategies might be of value to you? List/discuss.

Answer key:
1. B   2. C   3. B   4. C   5. C   6. B   7. C   8. B   9. C
Source: California Department of Motor Vehicles. Laws in other states may vary.

Reading Reasons: Motivational Mini-Lessons for Middle and High School. Kelly Gallagher. Copyright © 2003. Stenhouse Publishers.

Want to Get Your Driver's License?

Here is a practice Department of Motor Vehicles exam. Drivers must take and pass a written exam to obtain a driver's license. See how you do!

1. Which of the following statements about blind spots is true?
   (A) They are eliminated if you have one outside mirror on each side of the vehicle.
   (B) Large trucks have bigger blind spots than most passenger vehicles.
   (C) Blind spots can be checked by looking in your rearview mirror.

2. You are about to make a left turn. You must signal continuously during the last _____ feet before the turn.
   (A) 50
   (B) 75
   (C) 100

3. When parking uphill on a two-way street with no curbs, your front wheels should be:
   (A) turned to the left (toward the street).
   (B) turned to the right (away from the street).
   (C) parallel with the pavement.

4. Roadways are the most slippery:
   (A) during a heavy downpour.
   (B) after it has been raining for a while.
   (C) the first rain after a dry spell.

5. When driving in fog, you should use your:
   (A) fog lights only.
   (B) high beams.
   (C) low beams.

6. To avoid last-minute moves, you should be looking down the road to where your vehicle will be in about:
   (A) 5 to 10 seconds.
   (B) 10 to 15 seconds.
   (C) 15 to 20 seconds.

7. A school bus ahead of you in your lane is stopped with red lights flashing. You should:
   (A) stop, then proceed when you think all the children have exited the bus.
   (B) slow to 25 MPH and pass cautiously.
   (C) stop as long as the red lights are flashing.

8. A white painted curb means it's a:
   (A) loading zone for freight or passengers.
   (B) loading zone for passengers or mail only.
   (C) loading zone for freight only.

9. You may legally block an intersection:
   (A) when you entered the intersection on a green light.
   (B) during rush hour traffic.
   (C) under no circumstances.

(*Source:* California Department of Motor Vehicles)

MINI-LESSON
13

Reading Is
Rewarding

Reading
Builds a
Mature
Vocabulary

Reading
Makes You a
Better Writer

Reading Is
Hard, and
"Hard" Is
Necessary

Reading
Makes You
Smarter

Reading
Prepares You
for the World
of Work

Reading Well
Is Financially
Rewarding

Reading
Opens the
Door to
College and
Beyond

Reading Arms
You Against
Oppression

An Educated Electorate

One place where hard reading is necessary is the voting booth. Ballot measures and propositions are often loaded with legalese—so much so that careful reading is often required *prior* to stepping into the voting booth. Close reading of the ballot ensures that we make an educated vote. Let's not forget George Orwell's classic, *1984*, where the ignorant citizenry of Oceania, the "proles," are abused and taken advantage of by their government. Big Brother makes ridiculous claims, and the proles, who are saturated in lottery fever, pornography, alcohol, sports, and propaganda, are unable to see the manipulation of their leaders. Orwell's book is prophetic; history has repeatedly shown that an uneducated citizenry is susceptible to hegemony. I frequently remind myself that my students are future voters, and it is in everyone's best interest if they enter the voting booth with critical reading skills.

1. In small groups, have students consider the questions in this chart:

What are the advantages of having an educated voting electorate?	What are the disadvantages of having an ignorant electorate?

2. Explain to students that frequently there are important measures on the ballot, and these measures often require difficult reading in order for one to vote intelligently. California's Proposition 209 initiative is one such example.

3. Pass out the text of Proposition 209 (or substitute the text of a local ballot issue). Have students read the text. Each group should answer the following questions: (1) If I vote yes on 209, what am I voting for? and (2) If I vote against 209, what am I voting against? Share and compare answers.

4. Possible follow-up reflections:

- Which is worse: not voting at all or voting in an uninformed way?
- Why is it important to read the ballot carefully?
- How does one get good at reading ballots?
- What happens to a citizenry that doesn't vote?

Reading Reasons: Motivational Mini-Lessons for Middle and High School. Kelly Gallagher. Copyright © 2003. Stenhouse Publishers.

Proposition 209: Text of Proposed Law

This initiative is submitted to the people in accordance with the provisions of Article II, Section 8 of the Constitution.

This initiative measure expressly amends the Constitution by adding a section thereto; therefore, new provisions proposed to be added are printed in italic type to indicate that they are new.

Section 31 is added to Article I of the California Constitution as follows:

SEC. 31. *(a) The state shall not discriminate against, or grant preferential treatment to, any individual or group on the basis of race, sex, color, ethnicity, or national origin in the operation of public employment, public education, or public contracting.*

(b) This section shall apply only to action taken after the section's effective date.

(c) Nothing in this section shall be interpreted as prohibiting bona fide qualifications based on sex which are reasonably necessary to the normal operation of public employment, public education, or public contracting.

(d) Nothing in this section shall be interpreted as invalidating any court order or consent decree which is in force as of the effective date of this section.

(e) Nothing in this section shall be interpreted as prohibiting action which must be taken to establish or maintain eligibility for any federal program, where ineligibility would result in a loss of federal funds from the state.

(f) For the purposes of this section, "state" shall include, but not necessarily be limited to, the state itself, any city, county, city and county, public university system, including the University of California, community college district, school district, special district, or any other political subdivision or government instrumentality of or within the state.

(g) The remedies available for violations of this section shall be the same, regardless of the injured party's race, sex, color, ethnicity, or national origin, as are otherwise available for violations of then-existing California antidiscrimination law.

(h) This section shall be self-executing. If any part or parts of this section are found to be in conflict with federal law or the United States Constitution, the section shall be implemented to the maximum extent that federal law and the United States Constitution permit. Any provision held invalid shall be severable from the remaining portions of this section.

Reading Is
Rewarding

Reading
Builds a
Mature
Vocabulary

Reading
Makes You a
Better Writer

Reading Is
Hard, and
"Hard" Is
Necessary

Reading
Makes You
Smarter

Reading
Prepares You
for the World
of Work

Reading Well
Is Financially
Rewarding

Reading
Opens the
Door to
College and
Beyond

Reading Arms
You Against
Oppression

The Fine Print

Sometimes reading hard stuff is necessary, especially when it comes to something we are all confronted with at one time or another—fine print. For example, it's probably safe to say that most of our students will someday purchase a cell phone. Buying a cell phone is one thing; understanding the terms you just agreed to is another.

1. Ask students why companies use fine print.

2. Have the students read the fine print for the cell phone advertisement. Ask students to write down the things they understand about the fine print. Have them list the main points.

3. Ask students to write questions they might still have about the terms of the cell phone agreement.

4. Share and discuss the questions the students still have.

5. Brainstorm other places students might encounter fine print in their lives.

What I understand about the fine print	Questions I still have about the fine print	Where else will I see fine print in my life?

Reading Reasons: Motivational Mini-Lessons for Middle and High School. Kelly Gallagher. Copyright © 2003. Stenhouse Publishers.

In bold red letters the newspaper ad for the new cell phone looks like a great deal. It promises 3,500 total monthly minutes plus 250 mobile-to-mobile minutes. In much smaller letters the ad defines the promised 3,500 minutes as 300 anytime minutes plus 3,200 night and weekend minutes. The mobile-to-mobile minutes apply only if the minutes are between customers of the same cell phone carrier. At the very bottom of the advertisement, in extremely small print, are the following conditions (though the ad is 14 inches tall, all of the fine print is confined to the bottom 3/4 inch):

Subject to service agreement and calling plan. $35 activation fee on primary line, up to $175 early termination fee per line. Taxes, other charges, and restrictions apply. Requires credit approval. Cannot combine with other offers or business plans. If exceed allowed minutes, standard airtime rates apply. Usage rounded up to the next full minute. Unused allowances lost. Requires CDMA equipment. Available in select markets. Service not available in all areas. Mobile-to-mobile: for calls on our network within your local mobile-to-mobile airtime rate area. Call forwarding, voice mail, calls to/from prepay customers excluded. Night and weekend: Nights 8:01 P.M.–5:59 A.M. M–F; Wknds 12:00 A.M. Sat.–11:59 P.M. Sun. Phone offer: California sales tax calculated on unactivated price. Overnight delivery where available. Offer expires January 31, 2002.

Reading Reasons: Motivational Mini-Lessons for Middle and High School. Kelly Gallagher. Copyright © 2003. Stenhouse Publishers.

Reading Is
Rewarding

Reading
Builds a
Mature
Vocabulary

Reading
Makes You a
Better Writer

Reading Is
Hard, and
"Hard" Is
Necessary

Reading
Makes You
Smarter

Reading
Prepares You
for the World
of Work

Reading Well
Is Financially
Rewarding

Reading
Opens the
Door to
College and
Beyond

Reading Arms
You Against
Oppression

Phone Home

Congratulations! Now that you were able to read through the contract details of your new cell phone, you may need even stronger reading skills to get it fully operational (especially with all the features on today's phones). You will find on the accompanying page, for example, the actual instructions for setting up the calling card option on your new cellular phone.

1. Have students read the instructions on how to set up the calling card option on their new cell phone.

2. Have students generate questions regarding what they still do not understand about the set-up procedure.

3. Share the questions and possible answers to these questions in small groups. Clarify misunderstanding(s).

4. Have each group brainstorm other examples in their future where they might have to read technical directions (examples: installing a new DVD player, installing new spark plugs in your car) or where they might need to read how-to-assemble directions (examples: putting together a new TV cabinet, assembling a new baby crib).

5. For homework, have students search for good examples of hard reading. Have students bring in examples of technical directions or assembly instructions. Have students bring an original copy and a photocopy.

6. The next day, share the hard reading in small groups.

7. Create a bulletin board headed "Reading Is Hard, and 'Hard' Is Necessary." Using the photocopies brought by students, make a collage of the difficult technical reading we are confronted with.

8. After constructing the bulletin board for students to see, have the students write their reflections. Possible topics:

   • Is developing the ability to read hard stuff important in today's society?
   • How do we get better at reading hard stuff?
   • What are specific reading strategies that can be used to make sense of this type of writing?
   • What is the cost of not being able to read technical material?

Reading Reasons: Motivational Mini-Lessons for Middle and High School. Kelly Gallagher. Copyright © 2003. Stenhouse Publishers.

Calling Card Set-Up Instructions

If you wish to use a calling card for long distance calls on your new cellular phone, you must first set up your calling card information. Your phone can save information from two calling cards.

Saving calling card information:

1. Press Menu 4 1 3.
2. Scroll to the desired calling card, then press Options.
3. Scroll to Edit, then press OK.
4. Enter your security code (see page 51), then press OK.
5. At Dialing sequence, press Select. Press down "V" to choose the dialing sequence your card uses, then press Select.

Dialing sequence	Use for cards that require you to:	Cards using this sequence
Access # + phone # + card #	Dial 1-800 access number, then phone number, then card number (+ PIN if required)	MCI, AT&T, True Choice, Sprint Canada, Unitel
Access # + card # + Phone #	Dial 1-800 access number, then card number (+ PIN if required), then phone number	NetworkMCI, WorldPhone, MCI
Prefix + phone # + card #	Dial the prefix (any numbers that must precede the phone number) and phone number you want to dial, then card number (+ PIN if required)	GTE, PacBell, AT&T, Stentor

Note: the order of the following steps may vary, depending on which dialing sequence your card uses. This procedure might not work well with all calling cards.

6. Enter access number (usually the 1-800 number listed on the back of the calling card) then press OK.
7. Enter your card number and/or PIN, then press OK. Your phone will display Save changes? Press OK.
8. Press down "V" to reach Card name, then press Select. Enter the card name using your phone's keypad, then press OK.

(*Source:* Nokia 5160 manual)

MINI-LESSON

16

Reading Is
Rewarding

Reading
Builds a
Mature
Vocabulary

Reading
Makes You a
Better Writer

Reading the World

Those who have the ability to read difficult text are at a distinct advantage in this information age in which we live. The ability to read hard stuff may save you money (examples: before you sign a car loan, shopping for home interest rates). It might also protect your health: one recent study, for example, found that people with little or no education are much more likely to misread their medical prescriptions, thus endangering themselves. Reading hard text is a necessary life skill.

1. For homework, have students read the law firm's notification on the facing page and list the main ideas for each of the five paragraphs.

Main ideas Paragraph 1	Main Ideas Paragraph 2	Main Ideas Paragraph 3	Main Ideas Paragraph 4	Main Ideas Paragraph 5

Reading
Makes You
Smarter

Reading
Prepares You
for the World
of Work

2. The next day in class, have students meet in small groups to share, discuss, and clear up any questions about the text. Why is it important for people who have taken Meridia to be able to read this notice?

3. Possible discussion/reflection items:

   - Is being able to read difficult text an advantage in our society?
   - List other examples where being able to read difficult text might save you time or money, or might protect your health.

Reading Well
Is Financially
Rewarding

Reading
Opens the
Door to
College and
Beyond

Reading Arms
You Against
Oppression

Reading Reasons: Motivational Mini-Lessons for Middle and High School. Kelly Gallagher. Copyright © 2003. Stenhouse Publishers.

The makers of the drug Meridia are being sued in a class action lawsuit. Some are claiming the drug is harmful. Read the following notice posted on the Internet by a law firm:

FDA Petitioned to Ban Abbott Drug Meridia: Drug Related to 33 Deaths and Hundreds of Injuries

On March 27, 2002, Schiffrin & Barroway, LLP filed a national class action lawsuit in New Jersey on behalf of all persons who were prescribed the weight loss drug Sibutramine, also known as Meridia (Reductil outside the United States). As alleged in the complaint, Abbott Laboratories, Inc., USA, Knoll Pharmaceuticals Co., BASF Corporation and BASF Pharma are named as the defendants in this action due to their responsibility in manufacturing, promoting, marketing, distributing, and selling Meridia. The drug was originally manufactured and distributed in New Jersey. The class action seeks to (1) inform the public that users and consumers of Meridia are at an increased risk of harm and/or death, (2) establish a medical monitoring fund so that every consumer may be tested and treated for the adverse effects of Meridia, (3) reimburse monies paid for the product, (4) provide compensation to all victims for personal injuries and death.

On March 19, 2002, a consumer watchdog group, Public Citizen, petitioned the Food and Drug Administration (FDA) to ban the anti-obesity medication Meridia, linking the drug to 29 deaths in the United States and four in Europe and almost 400 adverse reactions from use of the drug.

Meridia was initially developed as an anti-depressant, but during the initial development of the drug, Knoll noted that Meridia had an ability to produce weight loss and in 1990, Knoll began testing Meridia specifically as an anti-obesity agent. On September 26, 1996, the FDA advisory committee declined to recommend approval of Meridia, claiming that "Sibutramine has an unsatisfactory risk-benefit ratio and, therefore, this reviewer recommends non-approval of the original submission." The committee also expressed concern about blood pressure increase experienced by study participants. Following the FDA's initial disapproval, Knoll pushed for fast track approval. In 1997, the Food and Drug Administration (FDA) did approve Meridia, calling it "moderately effective" at helping patients lose weight. Today, worldwide, Meridia is marketed in seventy (70) countries and sold as Reductil in Europe. It is estimated that 8.5 million people globally have taken Meridia since its approval. An estimated 2 million people in the United States currently take the medication.

Schiffrin & Barroway, LLP has extensive experience in handling class action litigation, including drug litigation, such as our recent involvement in the nationwide Baycol class action litigation. Attorneys in our firm are prepared to assist those who have endured injuries and suffering from taking this reportedly unsafe supplement, and are ready to help those with questions about the effects of this supplement on their health in the future.

If you or a family member have taken Meridia and developed any of the symptoms reported above, or are concerned about the potential effect this supplement can have on your body in the future, please call our office toll-free and speak with one of our attorneys at 1-888-299-7706.

(*Source:* Schiffrin & Barroway, LLP)

Reading Reasons: Motivational Mini-Lessons for Middle and High School. Kelly Gallagher. Copyright © 2003. Stenhouse Publishers.

Uncle Sam Wants You!

Reading Is
Rewarding

Reading
Builds a
Mature
Vocabulary

Reading
Makes You a
Better Writer

Reading Is
Hard, and
"Hard" Is
Necessary

Reading
Makes You
Smarter

Reading
Prepares You
for the World
of Work

Reading Well
Is Financially
Rewarding

Reading
Opens the
Door to
College and
Beyond

Reading Arms
You Against
Oppression

Often in our lives we are asked to read materials that have direct repercussions on our lives. From tax forms to lawsuits, from jury duty notices to contracts, our ability to read these materials accurately allows us to make educated decisions—decisions that may protect us from harm, save us hard-earned money, safeguard our health, or prevent us from wasting time and effort.

1. Give students the Selective Service chart, but block out the answers to the "Required to Register?" column. Have students predict who has to register and who doesn't by writing "yes" or "no" for each category.

Category	Required to register?
Military-related	
Active military duty	No*
Men attending service academies, like the U.S. Air Force Academy	No*
Men attending the U.S. Coast Guard Academy	No*
Men attending the Merchant Marine Academy	Yes
Men in military officer procurement programs	No*
Members of the National Guard or Reserves not on duty	Yes
Delayed Entry Program enlistees	Yes
Men who separate from active military duty before they turn 26	Yes
Men rejected for enlistment for any reason before turning 26	Yes
Aliens**	
Lawful non-immigrants on visas	No
Permanent resident aliens	Yes
Special (seasonal) agricultural workers (Form I-688)	Yes
Special agricultural workers (Form I-688A)	No
Refugee, parolee aliens	Yes
Undocumented (illegal) aliens	Yes
Confined	
Incarcerated, hospitalized, or institutionalized for medical reasons	No*
Handicapped physically or mentally	
Able to function in public with or without assistance	Yes
Continually confined to a residence, hospital, or institution	No

*Must register within 30 days of release unless already age 26, already registered when released, or exempt during entire period age 18 through 25.

**Immigrants who did not enter the United States or maintained their lawful non-immigrant status by continually remaining on a valid visa until after they were 26 years old were never required to register. Also, immigrants born before 1960 who did not enter the United States or maintained their lawful non-immigrant status by continually remaining on a valid visa until after March 29, 1975 were never required to register.

Note: Residents of Puerto Rico, Guam, Virgin Islands, and Northern Mariana Islands are U.S. citizens. Citizens of American Samoa are nationals and must register when their permanent address is in the U.S.

2. Have students share answers in small groups.

3. Have students read the footnotes and summarize each of them in their own words.

4. Ask students why it is important to be able to accurately read this chart. Brainstorm the following list: What will be the five most important things I will have to read in my life? Share responses.

Reading Reasons: Motivational Mini-Lessons for Middle and High School. Kelly Gallagher. Copyright © 2003. Stenhouse Publishers.

Selective Service: Who Must Register?

Almost all male U.S. citizens, regardless of where they live, and male immigrant aliens residing in the United States are required to be registered with Selective Service if they are at least 18 years old but not yet 26 years old. Men who are 26 years old and older are too old to register. Refer to the chart below to determine who is required by law to register for Selective Service:

Category	Required to register?
Military-related	
Active military duty	
Men attending service academies, like the U.S. Air Force Academy	
Men attending the U.S. Coast Guard Academy	
Men attending the Merchant Marine Academy	
Men in military officer procurement programs	
Members of the National Guard or Reserves not on duty	
Delayed Entry Program enlistees	
Men who separate from active military duty before they turn 26	
Men rejected for enlistment for any reason before turning 26	
*Aliens***	
Lawful non-immigrants on visas	
Permanent resident aliens	
Special (seasonal) agricultural workers (Form I-688)	
Special agricultural workers (Form I-688A)	
Refugee, parolee aliens	
Undocumented (illegal) aliens	
Confined	
Incarcerated, hospitalized, or institutionalized for medical reasons	
Handicapped physically or mentally	
Able to function in public with or without assistance	
Continually confined to a residence, hospital, or institution	

*Must register within 30 days of release unless already age 26, already registered when released, or exempt during entire period age 18 through 25.

**Immigrants who did not enter the United States or maintained their lawful non-immigrant status by continually remaining on a valid visa until after they were 26 years old were never required to register. Also, immigrants born before 1960 who did not enter the United States or maintained their lawful non-immigrant status by continually remaining on a valid visa until after March 29, 1975 were never required to register.

Note: Residents of Puerto Rico, Guam, Virgin Islands, and Northern Mariana Islands are U.S. citizens. Citizens of American Samoa are nationals and must register when their permanent address is in the U.S.

(*Source:* Selective Service Systems)

MINI-LESSON
18

Reading Is
Rewarding

Reading
Builds a
Mature
Vocabulary

Reading
Makes You a
Better Writer

Reading Is
Hard, and
"Hard" Is
Necessary

Reading
Makes You
Smarter

Reading
Prepares You
for the World
of Work

Reading Well
Is Financially
Rewarding

Reading
Opens the
Door to
College and
Beyond

Reading Arms
You Against
Oppression

You Are What You Eat

It never ceases to amaze me when a student shows up in my first-period class munching on a bag of potato chips and drinking a 44-ounce soda from the corner convenience store—all before 8:00 A.M! Seeing this makes me think that one real-world reading skill students need to develop is the ability to read nutritional labels!

1. Show students the nutritional information from two popular mystery cereals. Do not reveal the names of the cereals.

2. Ask students which cereal is more nutritious, cereal 1 or cereal 2.

3. In small groups have students discuss the two cereals and generate a list of why one cereal is better for you than the other.

4. Have each group share its list.

5. Have students reflect on this exercise. Possible topics:

   - Is the nutritional information easy to understand? Is some information difficult to understand?
   - What nutritional information is missing? (examples: total fat, cholesterol, carbohydrates)
   - Do you ever read food labels? If yes, when? where? why? If not, why not?
   - Why is it important to be able to read food labels?
   - Why does the government require food labels?
   - What are the possible consequences of never reading labels?

Answer key:
Mystery cereal 1: Cheerios
Mystery cereal 2: Lucky Charms

Reading Reasons: Motivational Mini-Lessons for Middle and High School. Kelly Gallagher. Copyright © 2003. Stenhouse Publishers.

Here are the nutritional facts for two leading breakfast cereals:

Mystery Cereal 1
Ingredients

- Whole grain oats (includes the oat bran)
- Modified cornstarch
- Wheat starch
- Sugar
- Salt
- Calcium carbonate
- Oat fiber
- Trisodium phosphate
- Vitamin E (mixed tocopherols) added to preserve freshness

Dietary fiber: 11%
Sugars: 1g
Protein: 3g

Mystery Cereal 2
Ingredients

- Whole grain oats (includes the oat bran)
- Marshmallow bits (sugar, modified cornstarch, corn syrup, dextrose, gelatin, calcium carbonate, artificial flavor, Yellows 5 and 6, Red 40, Blue 1)
- Sugar
- Corn syrup
- Cornstarch
- Salt
- Calcium carbonate
- Color added
- Trisodium phosphate
- Vitamin E (mixed tocopherols) added to preserve freshness

Dietary fiber: 5%
Sugars: 13g
Protein: 2g

According to the information given, which cereal is healthier for you?

(*Source:* General Mills)

Reading Makes You Smarter

Reading Is
Rewarding ✓

Reading
Builds a
Mature
Vocabulary

Reading
Makes You a
Better Writer

Reading Is
Hard, and
"Hard" Is
Necessary

Reading
Makes You
Smarter

Reading
Prepares You
for the World
of Work

Reading Well
Is Financially
Rewarding

Reading
Opens the
Door to
College and
Beyond

Reading Arms
You Against
Oppression

Brain Maintenance

Last night I umpired a girls' fast-pitch softball game. Today my legs are reminding me that I am not twenty-one years old anymore. Having to get in a crouch approximately 150 times to call balls and strikes has made me painfully aware of muscles in my legs I had forgotten I had. The soreness I'm experiencing today brings back the words of Mr. Patton, my junior high P.E. teacher: "Use your muscles or lose your muscles." When we don't use our muscles, they go soft. There is much research emerging that indicates the same holds true for our brain. If we don't use it, we run the risk of losing it. And reading remains one of the best exercises for keeping our brain sharp.

1. Ask students what happens to their muscles if they don't use them. Ask them to share examples of times they overdid it and paid the price with physical soreness.

2. Have students take the four-question Brain Maintenance Quiz. Have them discuss their answers and reasons in groups.

3. Discuss answers via a whole-class discussion.

4. Ask students to reflect on the importance reading plays in keeping one's brain sharp. Possible questions to spur reflection:

    *   Do you challenge yourself to learn new things?
    *   Do you read enough to keep your brain "muscle" strong?
    *   Do you watch too much television?
    *   What price will you pay later if you don't read now?

Answer key:
1. False. Researchers now believe your brain has the potential to grow throughout your life.
2. False. TV puts your brain in "neutral." Brain researchers suggest that you should turn the television off.
3. True. One study showed that those who read fewer books were more likely to develop problems as they aged.
4. True. Researchers now believe how much you read between the ages of six and eighteen are predictors of how well you'll think decades later.

Source for Brain Maintenance quiz: Lauran Neergaard

Reading Reasons: Motivational Mini-Lessons for Middle and High School. Kelly Gallagher. Copyright © 2003. Stenhouse Publishers.

Brain Maintenance Quiz

True or false?

1. Your brain stops growing after age five.

2. Television provides good brain exercise.

3. The lower your education level, the higher your chances may be that you will suffer from dementia later in life.

4. If you exercise your brain a lot when you are young, you build up reserves to fight brain problems later.

Helpful activities to keep your brain sharp as you age:

- Learn new hobbies.

- Study a new language.

- Do crossword puzzles.

- Play chess or other games.

- Read, read, read.

Reading Is
Rewarding

Reading
Builds a
Mature
Vocabulary

Reading
Makes You a
Better Writer

Reading Is
Hard, and
"Hard" Is
Necessary

Join the Million Word Club

Though direct vocabulary instruction is necessary, the primary strategy for acquiring new vocabulary is extensive reading. Students who read the most not only develop mature vocabularies, they also perform better on reading exams. In one study (Anderson, Wilson, and Fielding 1988), students who read ninety minutes a day scored in the 98th percentile on a standardized reading exam. These students, over the course of a year, read close to 5 million words—the most "bang for the buck" for acquiring vocabulary and for learning new ideas. Interestingly, students who read a mere twenty minutes a day will still read a million words a year.

Though this study measured the reading fluency of fifth-grade students, I have found the reading estimates to be fairly accurate for my high school seniors.

1. Write the word "scant" on the board or overhead and ask students to predict its meaning.

2. After students predict the meaning, write this sentence on the board or overhead: There were scant flowers left in the garden after the children picked them.

3. Have students revise their predictions after seeing the word in context. Most students will figure out what the word means.

4. Point out to students they have just learned one new word—scant—by reading only one sentence in five seconds. Ask students: What will happen to you if you read a million words?

5. Share and discuss the Amount of Time Spent Reading and Reading Achievement of Fifth Graders chart.

6. Create a chart as follows and have students complete and share:

My thoughts about this reading study	How will I benefit from reading a million words?

Reading
Prepares You
for the World
of Work

Reading Well
Is Financially
Rewarding

Reading
Opens the
Door to
College and
Beyond

Reading Arms
You Against
Oppression

Reading Reasons: Motivational Mini-Lessons for Middle and High School. Kelly Gallagher. Copyright © 2003. Stenhouse Publishers.

Amount of Time Spent Reading and
Reading Achievement of Fifth Graders

Percentile rank on reading tests	Minutes of reading per day	Estimated number of words read per year
98	90.7	4,733,000
90	40.4	2,357,000
70	21.7	1,168,000
50	12.9	601,000
20	3.1	134,000
10	1.6	51,000

(*Source:* Anderson, Wilson, and Fielding 1988)

MINI-LESSON

21

Reading Is
Rewarding

Reading
Builds a
Mature
Vocabulary

Reading
Makes You a
Better Writer

Reading Is
Hard, and
"Hard" Is
Necessary

Reading
Makes You
Smarter

Reading
Prepares You
for the World
of Work

Reading Well
Is Financially
Rewarding

Reading
Opens the
Door to
College and
Beyond

Reading Arms
You Against
Oppression

Read All About It!

It concerns me that most of my students do not read the newspaper. (It concerns newspaper publishers as well, because readership is dying off.) In fact, many of my students do not receive any kind of news, via the newspaper or any other media. This lesson is designed to allow students to see the value of becoming a regular newspaper reader. The list here is generated from the February 24, 2002, edition of the *Los Angeles Times;* a similar list could be generated from any newspaper on any given day.

1. Generate and share with students a list of what you learned in today's newspaper.

2. Give students copies of today's newspaper and give them time to look it over. Have them list fifteen things they learned in today's newspaper and share the information in groups.

3. Have students consider why they should become daily newspaper readers. How will their lives benefit?

Things I learned in today's newspaper	How will reading a newspaper regularly influence my life?
1. 2. 3. 4. 5. 6. 7. 8. 9. 10. 11. 12. 13. 14. 15.	

Consider
If you have a computer lab with Internet access, students could do this mini-lesson reading a major newspaper located somewhere out-of-state.

Reading Reasons: Motivational Mini-Lessons for Middle and High School. Kelly Gallagher. Copyright © 2003. Stenhouse Publishers.

15 Things I Learned from Today's Newspaper

1. For the first time ever, people bought more blank CDs last year than all music albums. Music executives are worried about future sales.

2. Sweden is about to approve a bill that will allow gay couples to adopt children.

3. Macy's is having a 65% off clothing sale this weekend.

4. The Auto Show is opening next month at the Convention Center. Tickets: $7.

5. Today will be mostly sunny, high around 73 degrees. Sunrise was at 6:26 A.M. Sunrise will be at 5:44 P.M.

6. The United States' men's bobsled team broke a forty-six-year drought by winning silver and bronze medals yesterday.

7. There is a women's professional football league. California will play Florida in the championship game.

8. The Washington Monument is now reopened for tourists.

9. What time *Lord of the Rings* is playing at the theater, and where to get tickets to see the theatrical version of *The Lion King*.

10. Predictions of who will win the upcoming Grammy awards.

11. A mansion in Beverly Hills is available to interested buyers. All you need is $19.5 million.

12. President Bush is proposing that we drill in Alaska for oil.

13. Author Patricia Cornwell is coming out with a book in which she claims she now knows the identity of the mysterious Jack the Ripper.

14. What my patient's rights are when I visit the doctor.

15. How to save a dollar next time I purchase Honey Nut Cheerios.

(*Source: Los Angeles Times,* Feb. 24, 2002)

MINI-LESSON

22

Reading Is
Rewarding

Reading
Builds a
Mature
Vocabulary

Reading
Makes You a
Better Writer

Reading Is
Hard, and
"Hard" Is
Necessary

Rustproofing

I have coached a number of high school basketball teams, and they all had one thing in common: whenever they had any time off from practice the players became rusty. Monday practices were always the hardest because the players, returning from being off for a day or two, had lost a bit of sharpness. Like basketball players, students who do not read daily become rusty at the skill of reading. This is why it is often difficult to get students to read silently for any length of time in early September. They are out of reading shape.

1. Have students estimate how much time they might spend reading during a five-year span. To do this:

   * Ask each student to estimate how many minutes of reading he or she has done during the past seven days.
   * Multiply that number by 52 to estimate how many minutes each student might read in a year.
   * Divide minutes by 60 to get an hour total.
   * Multiply by 5 to estimate how many hours each student might read in a five-year period.

2. In small groups, and then as an entire class, share some of the responses. Note the range of reading totals.

3. Share the Practice Adds Up chart with the students. Individually, or in small groups, have the students discuss or write what the chart means.

4. Have the students reflect on the chart, their reading estimate, and the implications of practicing daily versus weekly.

Consider
Repeat this entire lesson, but instead of charting reading time, have students chart time spent watching television. Determine how much television they watch in a five-year period. Compare total television viewing time with time spent reading.

Reading
Makes You
Smarter

Reading
Prepares You
for the World
of Work

Reading Well
Is Financially
Rewarding

Reading
Opens the
Door to
College and
Beyond

Reading Arms
You Against
Oppression

Reading Reasons: Motivational Mini-Lessons for Middle and High School. Kelly Gallagher. Copyright © 2003. Stenhouse Publishers.

Practice Adds Up

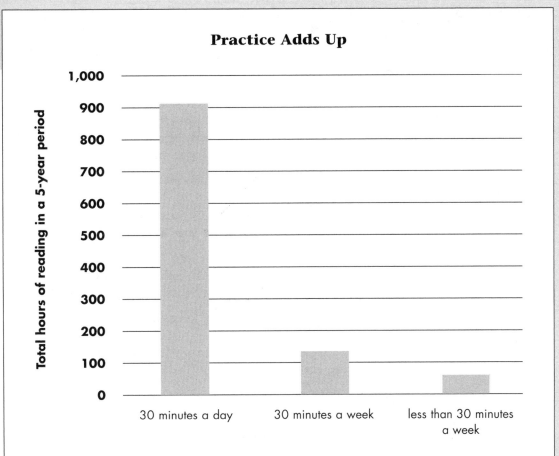

Total hours of reading in a 5-year period

| 30 minutes a day | 30 minutes a week | less than 30 minutes a week |

Over a five-year period, a person who reads 30 minutes a day will read 780 hours more than a person who reads 30 minutes a week!

MINI-LESSON

23

Reading Is
Rewarding

Reading
Builds a
Mature
Vocabulary

Reading
Makes You a
Better Writer

Reading Is
Hard, and
"Hard" Is
Necessary

Reading
Makes You
Smarter

Reading
Prepares You
for the World
of Work

Reading Well
Is Financially
Rewarding

Reading
Opens the
Door to
College and
Beyond

Reading Arms
You Against
Oppression

Who Scores Highest?

As the 1992 NAEP assessment illustrates, there is a strong relationship between how much print access students have, how frequently they read, and their reading achievement. Generally, students who had access to the most books and were given the most time to read scored the highest. Conversely, students who had the fewest number of books available and the least amount of time to read fared the worst.

1. Place students in small groups and distribute the NAEP chart to them. Give each group an overhead transparency along with a marker (if no overhead is available, butcher paper will suffice).

2. Ask students to read and discuss the chart. Ask them if they detect any trends or patterns to the information presented in the chart.

3. Tell each group they have seven minutes to determine the main point of this chart. Each group is to write a one-sentence thesis statement on their transparency. This statement should be a complete sentence and should capture the main idea of the study.

4. Choose a student at random from each group to present each group's thesis statements.

5. Have students complete the following:

My group's thesis statement	My thoughts/reaction

Reading Reasons: Motivational Mini-Lessons for Middle and High School. Kelly Gallagher. Copyright © 2003. Stenhouse Publishers.

NAEP Chart

State	NAEP reading rank	Average print access rank	Free reading rank
New Hampshire	1	7	5
Maine	2	10	22
Iowa	4	4	1
Massachusetts	4	13	5
North Dakota	4	2	9
Wisconsin	6	4	5
New Jersey	8	9	35
Wyoming	8	5	20
Connecticut	9	6	20
Indiana	16	11	27
Minnesota	16	8	2
Nebraska	16	1	7
Pennsylvania	16	17	7
Utah	16	18	13
Virginia	16	15	13
Idaho	17	22	23
Missouri	17	14	13
Oklahoma	17	23	33
Ohio	19	20	22
Colorado	21	21	9
Rhode Island	21	25	13
Michigan	23	16	14
West Virginia	23	32	39
New York	24	12	20
Delaware	26	31	33
Kentucky	26	38	41
Texas	26	39	33
Georgia	29	36	20
North Carolina	29	26	25
Tennessee	29	37	28
Arkansas	32	29	37
Maryland	32	19	24
New Mexico	32	34	36
South Carolina	34	30	33
Arizona	35	27	33
Florida	36	33	35
Alabama	37	41	41
Louisiana	38	28	38
Hawaii	39	25	20
California	40	40	20
Mississippi	41	42	42
District of Columbia	42	36	27

(*Source:* NCES 1994)

Reading Reasons: Motivational Mini-Lessons for Middle and High School. Kelly Gallagher. Copyright © 2003. Stenhouse Publishers.

MINI-LESSON

24

Reading Prepares You for the World of Work

Reading Is
Rewarding

Reading
Builds a
Mature
Vocabulary

Reading
Makes You a
Better Writer

Reading Is
Hard, and
"Hard" Is
Necessary

Reading
Makes You
Smarter

Reading
Prepares You
for the World
of Work

Reading Well
Is Financially
Rewarding

Reading
Opens the
Door to
College and
Beyond

Reading Arms
You Against
Oppression

Get a Job!

Students often do not see the relationship between developing their reading skills and progressing toward a meaningful career. The amount of reading done in most schools today is inadequate in its level of preparation. This chart reinforces the notion that most meaningful jobs require at least two years of post–high school education, if not more.

1. Share the Career Chart with the students.

2. Have students create a four-column chart, as shown below.

3. Have students brainstorm the four columns, choosing one job in the first column they believe to be attainable some day. In the second column, they list any education or training necessary to that occupation. In the third column, students consider the reading demands necessary to complete the training and to do the job successfully.

4. Ask students to reflect in the fourth column why reading now may benefit them in their future.

A sample student chart:

Possible future job	Education or training required	Reading demands	Why should I read now?
Firefighter	Two-year Fire Academy degree Ongoing specialized training	Physics Chemistry Fire codes Engineering text Medical/first aid Maps	(The student records his or her reflections here.)

Reading Reasons: Motivational Mini-Lessons for Middle and High School. Kelly Gallagher. Copyright © 2003. Stenhouse Publishers.

Career Chart

Two-year degree	Four-year degree (bachelor's degree)	More than four-year degree (master's degree or higher)
Computer technician	FBI agent	Lawyer
Surveyor	Engineer	Teacher
Registered nurse	Journalist	Doctor
Dental hygienist	Insurance agent	Architect
Medical lab technician	Pharmacist	University professor
Commercial artist	Computer analyst	Economist
Hotel manager	Dietician	Psychologist
Restaurant manager	Writer	Dentist
Engineering technician	Investment banker	Veterinarian
Automotive mechanic	Graphic designer	Geologist
Administrative assistant	Social worker	Zoologist
Plant operator	Public relations	Management consultant
Heating technician	Accountant	Public policy analyst
Air-conditioning technician		
Refrigeration technician		

"Most educators and business leaders agree that merely graduating from high school today is not enough to ensure economic success. To get a good job, students need at least a two- or four-year college degree."

(*Source: Los Angeles Times*)

Reading Reasons: Motivational Mini-Lessons for Middle and High School. Kelly Gallagher. Copyright © 2003. Stenhouse Publishers.

MINI-LESSON
25

Reading Is
Rewarding

Reading
Builds a
Mature
Vocabulary

Reading
Makes You a
Better Writer

Reading Is
Hard, and
"Hard" Is
Necessary

Reading
Makes You
Smarter

Reading
Prepares You
for the World
of Work

Reading Well
Is Financially
Rewarding

Reading
Opens the
Door to
College and
Beyond

Reading Arms
You Against
Oppression

Reading Demands of the Workplace

Based on their research of a number of major companies, Richard J. Murnane and Frank Levy, authors of *Teaching the New Basic Skills,* have determined the baseline reading demands of the modern workplace. Their findings are a bit scary: we are graduating hordes of students who do not read well enough to obtain and hold on to middle-class jobs. What was good-enough reading for a middle-class job twenty years ago is not good enough today. In short, the literacy demands of the workplace are rising.

1. For homework, give students the NAEP reading scores, the scoring key, and the quotation. Have them read them and come to class the next day with one written question and one written comment. These questions and comments may vary widely.

2. Upon returning to class the next day, have students converse in small groups, using their written questions and/or comments as a springboard for conversation.

3 If time permits, share as a whole class.

4. Have students write a reflection on one point made during their discussion.

5. Have students write a second short reflection addressing the following question: Do you think your reading level is at a level that will enable you to compete for middle-class jobs? If yes, why do you believe so? If no, what can you do to bring your reading skills up to the necessary level?

Reading Reasons: Motivational Mini-Lessons for Middle and High School. Kelly Gallagher. Copyright © 2003. Stenhouse Publishers.

Average NAEP Reading Scores, 1992, 1994, and 1996

	1992	1994	1996
All students	290	288	288
White	297	296	295
Black	261	266	266
Latino	271	263	265
Male	284	282	281
Female	296	295	295

Reading score range:

200 Can comprehend specific or sequentially related information

250 Can search for specific information, interrelate ideas, and make generalizations

300* Can find, understand, summarize, and explain relatively complicated information

350 Can synthesize and learn from specialized reading materials

*300 points or higher is the estimated NAEP reading score needed to earn a middle-class income today.

"Close to half of all 17-year-olds cannot read or do math at the level needed to get a job in a modern automobile plant. Barring some other special knowledge that would allow them to make a living as, say, a plumber or an artist, they lack the skills to earn a middle-class paycheck in today's economy."

(*Source:* Murnane and Levy 1996, p. 35)

MINI-LESSON
26

Reading Is
Rewarding

Reading
Builds a
Mature
Vocabulary

Reading
Makes You a
Better Writer

Reading Is
Hard, and
"Hard" Is
Necessary

Reading
Makes You
Smarter

Reading
Prepares You
for the World
of Work

Reading Well
Is Financially
Rewarding

Reading
Opens the
Door to
College and
Beyond

Reading Arms
You Against
Oppression

Reading Is Job One

Despite all the gloom and doom out there, there are a number of studies indicating that students today are actually reading at about the same levels as students thirty years ago (read Jeff McQuillan's *The Literacy Crisis* if you have doubts). That's the good news. The bad news is that the literacy demands of our society are not the same as they were thirty years ago. In fact, they are rising dramatically. Students leaving high school and college today will enter a workforce with more literacy demands than ever before. Students who read well will be better equipped to adapt to these rising literacy demands.

1. Share the chart with students, outlining how the reading demands of the school secretary have changed in the last thirty years.

2. After examining the changes secretaries have undergone in the last twenty years, ask students to predict what new kind of things secretaries will have to learn to read twenty years from now. Instead of looking back, have students look forward and predict.

3. Ask students to consider a job they might have twenty years from now. What will the literacy demands of that job be?

4. Eric Hoffer said, "In times of change, learners inherit the Earth, while the learned find themselves beautifully equipped to deal with a world that no longer exists." How do we remain "learners" instead of being simply "learned"? How does reading factor into remaining a learner? Have students write a reflection to Hoffer's quote and have students share in groups.

Reading Reasons: Motivational Mini-Lessons for Middle and High School. Kelly Gallagher. Copyright © 2003. Stenhouse Publishers.

Reading Is Job One

Reading demands of our school secretary, 1980s	Reading demands of our school secretary today
Memos	Memos
Handwritten notes	Handwritten notes
Typed papers	Typed papers
Typed inventories and budgets	Typed inventories and budgets
	E-mail
	Microsoft Office

- Word
- Excel
- PowerPoint
- Outlook

Internet

- Access other school districts
- Access county office
- Access research
- Transcripts
- Web sites

Calendar Maker

CD-roms

Stores (warehouse ordering system)

Bi-Tech (inventory tracking system)

Access (database)

Photoshop

Scanned materials

Clip art

Reading Reasons: Motivational Mini-Lessons for Middle and High School. Kelly Gallagher. Copyright © 2003. Stenhouse Publishers.

Reading Is
Rewarding

Reading
Builds a
Mature
Vocabulary

Reading
Makes You a
Better Writer

Reading Is
Hard, and
"Hard" Is
Necessary

Reading
Makes You
Smarter

**Reading
Prepares You
for the World
of Work**

Reading Well
Is Financially
Rewarding

Reading
Opens the
Door to
College and
Beyond

Reading Arms
You Against
Oppression

Sharpening Work Skills

The literacy demands of the workplace are increasing. Students who graduate with the ability to read and think critically will be at a marked advantage in the New Economy. Due to automation, the number of unskilled jobs in the marketplace has decreased significantly, and because of continued technological breakthroughs, the number of these jobs is expected to continue to dwindle. The next generation of unskilled workers runs a much higher chance of being unemployed than ever before in our nation's history.

1. Ask students to define the following job classifications: unskilled, skilled, and professional.

2. Have students generate specific job examples for each category.

3. In small groups, have students examine the Jobs in the United States chart. Have students track their conversation in the following chart:

What does the chart say?	What does the chart mean?
(Have them discuss the trend here.)	(Have them consider why this trend has occurred.)

4. Have students predict whether the trend will continue in the years they will be working. Write a reflection. Discuss in class.

Reading Reasons: Motivational Mini-Lessons for Middle and High School. Kelly Gallagher. Copyright © 2003. Stenhouse Publishers.

Define the following and give examples of each:

Unskilled job	Skilled job	Professional job

Jobs in the United States

Decade	Professional jobs	Skilled jobs	Unskilled jobs
1950s	20%	20%	60%
1990s	20%	60%	20%
2010	?	?	?

(*Source:* Murnane and Levy 1996)

Reading Well Is Financially Rewarding

Reading Is
Rewarding

Reading
Builds a
Mature
Vocabulary

Reading
Makes You a
Better Writer

Reading Is
Hard, and
"Hard" Is
Necessary

Reading
Makes You
Smarter

Reading
Prepares You
for the World
of Work

How Much Will You Be Paid for Attending Class Today?

Did you know that if you invested $25 a month into a savings account with 6 percent interest you would have saved $16,650 in ten years? The more you contribute over the years, the more you'll have to take out when you need the money. The same is true of school. Consider this class a big reading piggy bank. For every reading deposit students make, the better they'll read, the more education they'll receive, the better their chances will be for gaining lifelong financial independence.

1. Reveal the first three figures on the chart so the students can see the difference in earnings between high school graduates and non–high school graduates ($280,000).

2. Make sure students understand that their high school diploma is worth, on average, $280,000.

3. Present the students with the following problem: If a high school diploma is worth $280,000, how much are you being paid to attend this class period today? Here are some factors you'll need to consider to arrive at the correct answer:

   • High school is four years.
   • Each school year is approximately 180 days. We'll round that down to 175 days a year to allow for absences.
   • Each class day has 6 periods. (If your school schedule is different, you can adjust accordingly.)

4. Make the reading connection again to the students. The more you read, the longer students will be able to make yearly educational investments. Have students write a written reflection on this connection.

Reading Well
Is Financially
Rewarding

Reading
Opens the
Door to
College and
Beyond

Reading Arms
You Against
Oppression

Reading Reasons: Motivational Mini-Lessons for Middle and High School. Kelly Gallagher. Copyright © 2003. Stenhouse Publishers.

How Much Will You Be Paid to Attend This Class Today?

Students who finish high school earn $1,216,000

Students who do not finish high school earn . . . $936,000

This means attending high school pays $280,000

High school = 4 school years = approximately 700 days of school

$280,000 divided by 700 days = $400 per day of high school

Each school day has 6 periods. $400 divided by 6 = $66.67

You will be paid

$66.67*

to attend this class today!

---

*Actually, if you continue on to college or trade school, you'll make even more for attending this class today.

(A plumber, doctor, or auto mechanic doesn't ask to be paid before the job is finished. You shouldn't either!)

(*Source:* U.S. Census 2000)

Reading Reasons: Motivational Mini-Lessons for Middle and High School. Kelly Gallagher. Copyright © 2003. Stenhouse Publishers.

MINI-LESSON
29

Reading Is
Rewarding

Reading
Builds a
Mature
Vocabulary

Reading
Makes You a
Better Writer

Reading Is
Hard, and
"Hard" Is
Necessary

Reading
Makes You
Smarter

Reading
Prepares You
for the World
of Work

Making Bank

Unless you inherit a successful family business, win the state lottery, or discover sunken treasure, it is likely that your income will be closely related to the amount of education you achieve. Most of our students will earn more if they learn more. Most of our students will learn more if they read better. Most of our students will read better if they read more. Time spent reading now is a financial investment in the future.

1. Show students the chart U.S. Average Career Earnings for People 18 Years Old and Older. Keep the third column, "Actual career earnings," covered.

2. Have students predict the totals for each educational level.

3. Have students share predictions in small groups.

4. Uncover the actual figures in the third column.

5. If you have already done the mini-lesson "Raising a Child" (page 116), review it with students.

6. Have students reflect on one or more of the following possible questions:

   - What does this chart have to do with reading?
   - Are you reading enough to prepare for a future career?
   - Should you read more than you are currently reading?
   - How much money will you need to make in the future to support the kind of lifestyle you envision? How will developing your reading ability help you achieve your financial goals?

Reading Well
Is Financially
Rewarding

Reading
Opens the
Door to
College and
Beyond

Reading Arms
You Against
Oppression

Reading Reasons: Motivational Mini-Lessons for Middle and High School. Kelly Gallagher. Copyright © 2003. Stenhouse Publishers.

U.S. Average Career Earnings for People 18 Years Old and Older

(in millions of 1999 dollars)

Education level	Predicted career earnings	Actual career earnings
Less than high school diploma		$1.0
High school diploma		$1.2
Some college, no degree		$1.5
Associate degree		$1.6
Bachelor's degree		$2.1
Master's degree		$2.5
Doctoral degree		$3.4
Professional degree		$4.4

(*Source:* U.S. Census 2000)

Reading Reasons: Motivational Mini-Lessons for Middle and High School. Kelly Gallagher. Copyright © 2003. Stenhouse Publishers.

Reading Is
Rewarding

Reading
Builds a
Mature
Vocabulary

Reading
Makes You a
Better Writer

Reading Is
Hard, and
"Hard" Is
Necessary

Reading
Makes You
Smarter

Reading
Prepares You
for the World
of Work

**Reading Well
Is Financially
Rewarding**

Reading
Opens the
Door to
College and
Beyond

Reading Arms
You Against
Oppression

Nerds Win

Let's face it. Not many of us will grow up to be Michael Jordan or Bill Gates. Almost every one of us, however, will grow up needing a job. According to the U.S. Department of Labor, 90 percent of jobs today require either a technical education or a four-year college degree. Only 10 percent of jobs require unskilled labor. Unless your students become the next Michael Jordan, their reading abilities will become increasingly critical to their chances of making a decent living. Nerds will rule the roost in the New Economy.

1. Present the chart below and ask students to brainstorm the possible reading requirements for each of the listed occupations.

Occupation	Possible reading requirements
Teacher	Textbooks, memos, notes from parents, school board minutes, magazines, newspapers, grade books, bulletins, journals, books, reports, test scores, mail, catalogues . . .
Firefighter	
Auto mechanic	

2. In the blank box at the bottom of the chart, have the students choose an occupation they might be interested in pursuing one day and consider the reading requirements for that job.

3. Ask students how they can now begin preparing for that kind of reading.

Reading Reasons: Motivational Mini-Lessons for Middle and High School. Kelly Gallagher. Copyright © 2003. Stenhouse Publishers.

Is It Better to Be a Jock or a Nerd?

Michael Jordan makes $300,000 a game. That equals $10,000 a minute at an average of 30 minutes per game.

With $40 million in endorsements, he makes $178,100 a day, working or not.

If he sleeps seven hours a night, he makes $52,000 every night while visions of sugarplums are dancing in his head.

If he goes to see a movie, it'll cost him $8, but he'll make $18,550 while he's there.

If he decides to have a five-minute egg, he'll make $618 while boiling it.

He makes $7,414 an hour more than the minimum wage.

If he wants to save up for a new $90,000 Acura NSX, it will take him twelve hours.

If you were given a penny for every $10 he made, you'd be living comfortably at $65,000 a year.

This year, he'll make twice as much as all U.S. presidents for all their terms combined.

Amazing, isn't it?

However, if Jordan saves 100% of his income for the next 250 years, he'll still have less than Bill Gates has today.

Game over.

Nerd wins!

Do you think Bill Gates reads a lot?

MINI-LESSON
31

Reading Is
Rewarding

Reading
Builds a
Mature
Vocabulary

Reading
Makes You a
Better Writer

Reading Is
Hard, and
"Hard" Is
Necessary

Reading
Makes You
Smarter

Reading
Prepares You
for the World
of Work

Reading Well
Is Financially
Rewarding

Reading
Opens the
Door to
College and
Beyond

Reading Arms
You Against
Oppression

Raising a Child

Raising children is expensive. Though most students believe they will be parents one day, very few of them have stopped to think about the financial impact children will have on their lives. What's the connection to reading? More reading = more knowledge = more education = better job = more money = ability to provide for your children.

1. Ask your students how many of them might expect to be parents one day (if they're not parents already!).

2. Have students brainstorm a list of all the possible expenses a child incurs (clothing, food, medical, dance lessons, books, etc.).

3. Share in groups and create a whole-class list.

4. Ask students to predict the average cost of raising a child today.

5. Share the quote from the *Kansas City Star*.

6. Ask students the following: "What is the relationship between reading and the cost of raising a child?"

Expected expenses in raising a child	What is the relationship between reading and these expenses?

Reading Reasons: Motivational Mini-Lessons for Middle and High School. Kelly Gallagher. Copyright © 2003. Stenhouse Publishers.

Average Cost of Raising a Child Is $165,630

The average cost of raising a Y2K child for a middle-income family will be about $165,630—about $233,530 factoring in inflation—for food, shelter, and other necessities in the next seventeen years, according to an annual report released by the Agriculture Department.

(*Source: Kansas City Star,* June 13, 2001)

Reading Reasons: Motivational Mini-Lessons for Middle and High School. Kelly Gallagher. Copyright © 2003. Stenhouse Publishers.

MINI-LESSON
32

Reading Opens
the Door
to College
and Beyond

Reading Is
Rewarding

Reading
Builds a
Mature
Vocabulary

Reading
Makes You a
Better Writer

Reading Is
Hard, and
"Hard" Is
Necessary

Reading
Makes You
Smarter

Reading
Prepares You
for the World
of Work

Reading Well
Is Financially
Rewarding

Reading
Opens the
Door to
College and
Beyond

Reading Arms
You Against
Oppression

Getting in College Reading Shape

The California Education Round Table, comprised of the heads of the Department of Education, the University of California, the state colleges, and the community colleges, appointed a task force to issue a set of reading standards (known as the CERT standards). Developed in 2001 by California secondary and post-secondary faculty, administrators, and public representatives, these standards extensively detail the reading expectations of students entering college. This provides a reading target for our students, who will be better prepared for the reading rigors of college if they know ahead of time what the expectations will be. Though this was created by a task force in California, the identified skills needed for college are applicable to any university throughout the country.

1. Early in the school year, explain to students that a panel of college experts met and generated a list of reading skills they believe essential for students entering colleges and universities.

2. Share the list and have students score themselves in each category. Students should score each category between 1 and 10. A 10 indicates they do this specific skill very well. A 1 indicates they do not do that skill at all (or they don't understand the skill).

3. As the school year progresses, teach these specific skills.

4. Have students rescore themselves at the end of the school year.

5. As part of their portfolios or as a stand-alone reflection, have students write about their development as readers. Possible topics:

   - What are my strengths as a reader?
   - Where did I improve as a reader this year?
   - What are my weaknesses as a reader?
   - In which skill(s) do I need more practice?

Reading Reasons: Motivational Mini-Lessons for Middle and High School. Kelly Gallagher. Copyright © 2003. Stenhouse Publishers.

Skills Expected of Students Entering Colleges and Universities

Expected skill	My score (Sept.)	My score (June)
Read texts of complexity without instruction and guidance		
Summarize information		
Relate prior knowledge and experience to new information		
Make connections to related topics or information		
Synthesize information in discussion and written assignments		
Argue with the text		
Determine major and subordinate ideas in passages		
Anticipate where an argument or narrative is heading		
Suspend information while searching for answers to self-generated questions		
Identify the main idea		
Retain the information read		
Identify appeals made to the reader		
Identify the evidence that supports, confutes, or contradicts a thesis		
Read with awareness of self and others		

Score yourself:
10 = I do this very well.
 1 = I don't do this/I don't understand this at all.

(*Source:* California Education Round Table 2001)

MINI-LESSON

33

Reading Is
Rewarding

Reading
Builds a
Mature
Vocabulary

Reading
Makes You a
Better Writer

Reading Is
Hard, and
"Hard" Is
Necessary

Reading
Makes You
Smarter

Reading
Prepares You
for the World
of Work

Reading Well
Is Financially
Rewarding

Reading
Opens the
Door to
College and
Beyond

Reading Arms
You Against
Oppression

The Key to College

The road to college often travels through the SAT exam. I have found that even with junior high school students, it is beneficial for them to see the difficulty of the verbal section of the test. In this mini-lesson, I share one analogy question and one sentence completion question found on an actual SAT exam. Though students in junior high are not usually able to answer the questions correctly, they are able to see that they need to continue their development as readers so that when the real SAT rolls around, they will be prepared.

1. Have students read and attempt to answer the two questions.

2. Have students consider the following chart:

In the column below, list the skills a student needs to do well on these types of SAT questions.	Which of these skills are improved by reading a lot? (Place a check.)

A finished chart might look like this:

In the column below, list the skills a student needs to do well on these types of SAT questions.	Which of these skills are improved by reading a lot? (Place a check.)
Have a wide vocabulary	✓
Word attack skills	✓
Recognizing sentence structure	✓
Tap knowledge of synonyms, antonyms	✓
Consider prefixes, suffixes, roots	✓
Skim quickly	✓
Read around problems, consider context	✓

Answer key:
c, c

Reading Reasons: Motivational Mini-Lessons for Middle and High School. Kelly Gallagher. Copyright © 2003. Stenhouse Publishers.

The box below consists of a related pair of words or phrases, followed by five pairs of words or phrases labeled A through E. Select the pair that best expresses a relationship similar to that expressed in the original pair.

Illogical:Confusion::

(A)   profound:laughter

(B)   revolting:sympathy

(C)   astounding:amazement

(D)   obscure:contrast

(E)   deliberate:vitality

The sentence below has two blanks, each blank indicating something has been omitted. Beneath the sentence are five sets of words labeled A through E. Choose the set of words that, when inserted in the sentence, best fits the meaning of the sentence as a whole.

Even those who do not _____ Robinson's views _____ him as a candidate who has courageously refused to compromise his convictions.

(A)   shrink from . . . condemn

(B)   profit from . . . dismiss

(C)   concur with . . . recognize

(D)   disagree with . . . envision

(E)   dissent from . . . remember

(*Source: Ten Real SATs*)

Reading Reasons: Motivational Mini-Lessons for Middle and High School. Kelly Gallagher. Copyright © 2003. Stenhouse Publishers.

MINI-LESSON

34

Reading Is
Rewarding

Reading
Builds a
Mature
Vocabulary

Reading
Makes You a
Better Writer

Reading Is
Hard, and
"Hard" Is
Necessary

Reading
Makes You
Smarter

Reading
Prepares You
for the World
of Work

Reading Well
Is Financially
Rewarding

Reading
Opens the
Door to
College and
Beyond

Reading Arms
You Against
Oppression

The Road to Higher Learning

Sometimes students think college just magically "happens" after high school. They often enter ninth grade unaware of the specific hurdles they must overcome to gain acceptance to a college or university. Additionally, they may be oblivious to the importance reading plays in helping them successfully clear these hurdles.

1. Draw a "map" that shows the road between junior or senior high school and college. Ask students what hurdles they might encounter on this road. (Another visual that might work with your students: what are the hoops they must successfully jump through to gain college admission?) Have students draw and label the hurdles.

2. Have students brainstorm the reading demands of each hurdle (two examples below).

Hurdle	Reading demands
AP/honors classes	Close reading of college-level literature, poetry (English), formulas, equations (math, sciences), primary source documents (social science), reading and comprehending timed exams
Getting good grades/high school diploma	Daily and nightly reading of materials across the curriculum. Being able to read effectively in literature, biology, chemistry, physics, mathematics, and in a foreign language. Reading the following: • Functional materials: graphs, charts, maps • Consumer, workplace, and public documents • Instructional manuals • Online information • Speeches and essays • Periodicals (newspapers and magazines) Reading a great deal recreationally

Reading Reasons: Motivational Mini-Lessons for Middle and High School. Kelly Gallagher. Copyright © 2003. Stenhouse Publishers.

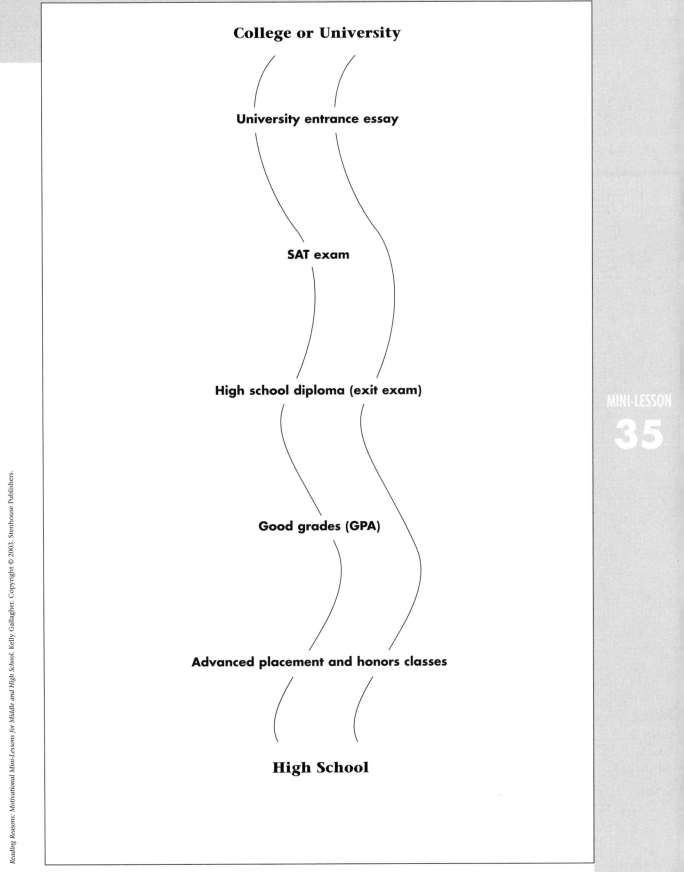

College or University

University entrance essay

SAT exam

High school diploma (exit exam)

Good grades (GPA)

Advanced placement and honors classes

High School

MINI-LESSON

35

Reading Is
Rewarding

Reading
Builds a
Mature
Vocabulary

Reading
Makes You a
Better Writer

Reading Is
Hard, and
"Hard" Is
Necessary

Reading
Makes You
Smarter

Reading
Prepares You
for the World
of Work

Reading Well
Is Financially
Rewarding

Survival of the Fittest

Despite more stringent entrance requirements, the competition to gain acceptance to our nation's prestigious colleges and universities has intensified in recent years. Last year at UCLA, for example, 7,731 applicants *with GPAs of 4.0 or higher* were denied admission! With such a fine line between who gets accepted and who doesn't, every tenth of a point of GPA or SAT score becomes critical. Those who read best have a distinct advantage.

1. Ask students to brainstorm a list of criteria college admission officers consider to determine which applicants are granted admission. The list should include the following: GPA, SAT scores, entrance essay, community service, and leadership qualities.

2. Have students rank these criteria in order of importance. Which factor, for example, is the first thing the admission officers consider? Rank them in perceived order of importance. My guess is that GPA and SAT will rank as most important (without strong grades and a strong SAT, the student's essay and experiences become moot).

3. Have students read the accompanying chart, Getting Accepted to a Prestigious University. In a three-minute quick write, have them react to the chart (they may react to a specific statistic or to the chart as a whole).

4. Ask the students if they think UCLA is an exception or if they think the competition is as intense at other prestigious universities. (UCLA is not an exception—competition is fierce at all esteemed universities.) Make the argument that at this level of competition every tenth of a point on their GPAs and on their SAT scores becomes critical.

5. If every tenth of a point becomes critical, how does reading factor into this competition? Follow-up questions to consider:

    *   How does reading for fun help us develop academically? (Consider many of the mini-lessons in this book, including "Don't Be Such a Borf," found on page 56.)
    *   Students who score the highest on the SAT verbal are usually the same students with the most reading experience. Why is this?
    *   How will reading a lot now help you later? How will it give you an edge when you enter the fierce competition for college admission?

Reading
Opens the
Door to
College and
Beyond

Reading Arms
You Against
Oppression

Reading Reasons: Motivational Mini-Lessons for Middle and High School. Kelly Gallagher. Copyright © 2003. Stenhouse Publishers.

Getting Accepted to a Prestigious University

(example: UCLA, 2002)

Number of students who applied to UCLA	43,421
Number of students admitted to UCLA	10,522
Number of students denied admission	32,314
Fully weighted GPAs of all who applied	3.83
Fully weighted GPAs of all admitted	4.23
SAT verbal average score of all who applied	582.6
SAT verbal average score of all admitted	642.3
4.0 GPAs or higher who were denied admission	7,731

(*Source:* Tracy Davis, UC Regent)

MINI-LESSON

36

Reading Arms You Against Oppression

Reading Is
Rewarding

Reading
Builds a
Mature
Vocabulary

Reading
Makes You a
Better Writer

Reading Is
Hard, and
"Hard" Is
Necessary

Reading
Makes You
Smarter

Reading
Prepares You
for the World
of Work

Reading Well
Is Financially
Rewarding

Reading
Opens the
Door to
College and
Beyond

Bridging the Digital Divide

In the past week, I have used my computer to find directions to a workshop, browse and order books, read the *New York Times* daily, purchase tickets to see *The Lion King,* comparison shop for softball equipment, research information for my class, check the ten-day weather forecast in Oakland (where I'll be attending a conference), read articles about the teaching of English, keep track of and schedule appointments, research Winter Olympics results, and write this paragraph you are now reading. The computer has become an indispensable tool in this information age, and the next generation of students without computer access will have a distinct disadvantage in developing their cultural literacy.

1. Ask students to consider all the possible uses of a computer. Brainstorm a list. Share your list with them.

2. Have the students read and analyze the Nationwide Percentage of Households with Computers information on the next page.

3. Ask students what kinds of reading advantages are gained by owning a computer.

4. Have students reflect on these advantages. Discuss.

Possible computer uses	Reading advantages	Your reflection

Reading Reasons: Motivational Mini-Lessons for Middle and High School. Kelly Gallagher. Copyright © 2003. Stenhouse Publishers.

The 2000 U.S. Census did more than count people. It collected valuable data about Americans' way of life. One question it asked was whether each household had a computer. The results might surprise you:

Nationwide Percentage of Households with Computers

By race:

Asian	65%
Black	33%
Hispanic	34%
White	53%

By income:

$20,000–$24,999	34%
$25,000–$34,999	47%
$35,000–$49,999	62%
$50,000–$74,999	75%

By education level:

Less than a high school diploma	18%
High school diploma	40%
Some college	60%
Bachelor's degree or more	76%

(*Source:* U.S. Census, 2000)

Reading Reasons: Motivational Mini-Lessons for Middle and High School. Kelly Gallagher. Copyright © 2003. Stenhouse Publishers.

MINI-LESSON

37

Reading Is
Rewarding

Reading
Builds a
Mature
Vocabulary

Reading
Makes You a
Better Writer

Reading Is
Hard, and
"Hard" Is
Necessary

Reading
Makes You
Smarter

Reading
Prepares You
for the World
of Work

Reading Well
Is Financially
Rewarding

Reading
Opens the
Door to
College and
Beyond

Reading Arms
You Against
Oppression

Closing the Achievement Gap

There is an achievement gap in this country, and it is along racial lines. Kati Haycock, in the March 2001 issue of *Educational Leadership,* notes that since 1988, this gap has widened. In 1999, by the end of high school, she adds, "only 1 in 50 Latinos and 1 in 100 African-American 17-year-olds can read and gain information from specialized text—such as the science section in the newspaper (compared to about 1 in 12 for whites), and fewer than one-quarter of Latinos and one-fifth of African-Americans can read the complicated but less specialized text that more than half of white students can read."

1. In small groups, have students discuss the chart Highest Educational Attainment for Every 100 Kindergartners.

2. Have students clear up any questions or misunderstandings via a whole-class discussion.

3. Have students draw and complete the following:

Possible reasons for this achievement gap	How does reading well help close this gap?

4. Have students discuss their responses to the second column.

Reading Reasons: Motivational Mini-Lessons for Middle and High School. Kelly Gallagher. Copyright © 2003. Stenhouse Publishers.

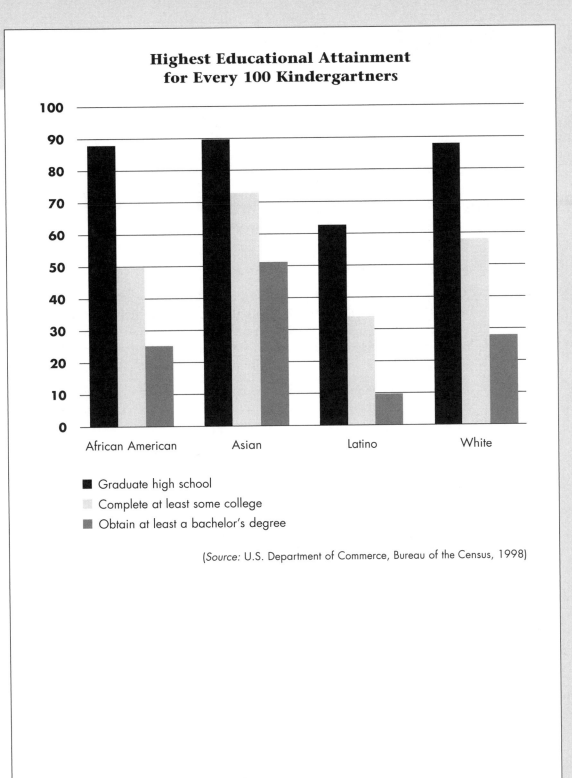

**Highest Educational Attainment
for Every 100 Kindergartners**

Legend:
- Graduate high school
- Complete at least some college
- Obtain at least a bachelor's degree

(*Source:* U.S. Department of Commerce, Bureau of the Census, 1998)

Reading Is
Rewarding

Reading
Builds a
Mature
Vocabulary

Reading
Makes You a
Better Writer

Reading Is
Hard, and
"Hard" Is
Necessary

Reading
Makes You
Smarter

Reading
Prepares You
for the World
of Work

Reading Well
Is Financially
Rewarding

Reading
Opens the
Door to
College and
Beyond

Reading Arms
You Against
Oppression

Fighting Poverty

Reading well in school not only has a positive effect on the life of students, it may also have a positive effect on the lives of *their* children as well. The reasoning goes something like this: the more our students read, the better they'll read. The better they read, the better they'll do in school. The better they perform in school, the longer they'll stay in school. The longer they stay in school, the more advanced their education will be. The more advanced their education, the less likely their own children will live in poverty. The ramifications of being able to read well extend far beyond the walls of any given classroom.

1. In small groups, distribute copies of the bar graph.

2. Ask students to decipher the meaning of this graph. What is its central message? Allow them a few minutes to discuss. Have them jot at least one thought from each group member in the left-hand column of the table below (as evidence they participated in the group discussion and have listened to every point of view).

3. In the middle column, have each group generate a thesis statement capturing the meaning of the graph. This should be written in one complete sentence.

Group notes for initial discussion	Thesis statement	Your thoughts (the reading connection)

4. Have each group orally share its thesis sentence.

5. After hearing all the groups discuss their thesis statements, have students write a reflection. How does reading play into this reflection?

Reading Reasons: Motivational Mini-Lessons for Middle and High School. Kelly Gallagher. Copyright © 2003. Stenhouse Publishers.

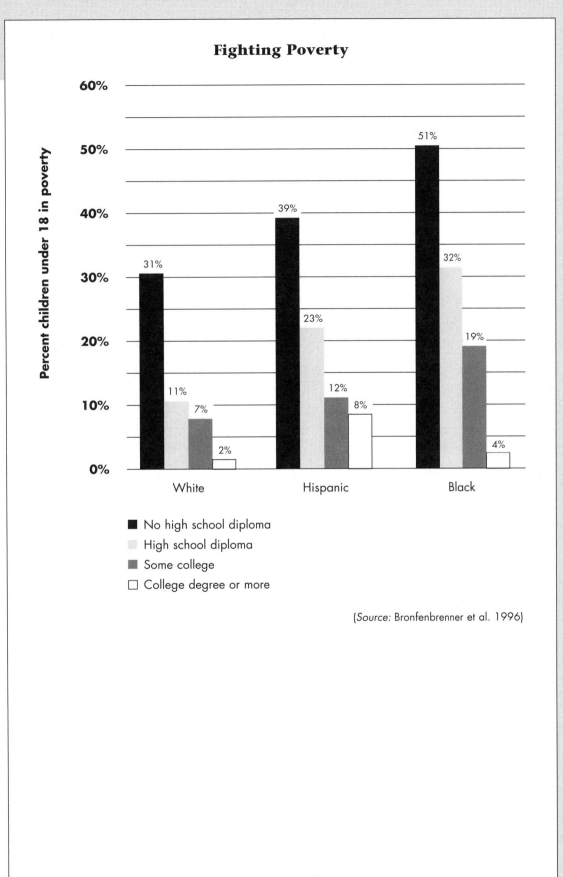

Fighting Poverty

Percent children under 18 in poverty

White
- No high school diploma: 31%
- High school diploma: 11%
- Some college: 7%
- College degree or more: 2%

Hispanic
- No high school diploma: 39%
- High school diploma: 23%
- Some college: 12%
- College degree or more: 8%

Black
- No high school diploma: 51%
- High school diploma: 32%
- Some college: 19%
- College degree or more: 4%

■ No high school diploma
☐ High school diploma
■ Some college
☐ College degree or more

(*Source:* Bronfenbrenner et al. 1996)

Reading Reasons: Motivational Mini-Lessons for Middle and High School. Kelly Gallagher. Copyright © 2003. Stenhouse Publishers.

MINI-LESSON
39

Reading Is
Rewarding

Reading
Builds a
Mature
Vocabulary

Reading
Makes You a
Better Writer

Reading Is
Hard, and
"Hard" Is
Necessary

Reading
Makes You
Smarter

Reading
Prepares You
for the World
of Work

Reading Well
Is Financially
Rewarding

Reading
Opens the
Door to
College and
Beyond

Reading Arms
You Against
Oppression

The More You Know . . .

The more you read, the more you will know in your life. The more you know, the less likely it will be that someone will take advantage of you. Voluminous reading serves as "rip-off" prevention. This connection—that reading strengthens our ability to fight oppression—is often invisible to students.

1. Give students the following sentence starter and ask them to predict its ending: "The more you read, _____."

2. Share student responses.

3. Unveil the entire first sentence: "The more you read, <u>the more you know.</u>"

4. Give students the next sentence starter and have them predict again: "The more you know, _____."

5. Repeat this process until all nine sentence starters are completed.

6. Upon completion of the sentence starters, have students reflect on which sentence is most meaningful to them and why (see chart below).

Sentence starter predictions	Which sentence starter is most meaningful and why?
1. The more you read, _____. 2. 3. 4. 5. 6. 7. 8. 9.	

Reading Reasons: Motivational Mini-Lessons for Middle and High School. Kelly Gallagher. Copyright © 2003. Stenhouse Publishers.

The More You Know . . .

1. The more you read, the more you know.

2. The more you know, the smarter you'll grow.

3. The smarter you are, the longer you'll stay in school and the more diplomas you'll earn.

4. The more diplomas you'll have, the more your children will achieve in school.

5. The more diplomas you'll have, the longer you will live.

6. The less you read, the less you'll know.

7. The less you know, the sooner you will drop out of school.

8. The sooner you drop out of school, the sooner and longer you'll be unemployed.

9. The sooner you drop out of school, the greater your chances are of being incarcerated.

(*Source:* Trelease 2001)

4

DEVELOPING YOUR OWN READING REASON LENS

A person who doesn't read is no better off than a person who can't read.
Mark Twain

While I hope that the forty mini-lessons found in this book will prove useful in helping your students discover the value of reading, I also hope that you, the teacher, see this book as a starting point in developing your own reading reasons. No one knows your students better than you, and your insights can be used to help develop your own lens—the ability to uncover reading reasons that will appeal to the specific needs and interests of your students.

For people who like to read, searching for reading reasons at first seems silly. We adults have already found a multitude of reasons to read. Sometimes we are conscious of these reasons; but often, I suspect, many of these reasons have become internalized. We often take them for granted because we have long ago acknowledged their value. We motivate ourselves to read, consciously or unconsciously, because the benefits of doing so are ingrained in us.

Unfortunately, this is not often the case with our students. Just because we have internalized a number of reasons why reading enriches our lives doesn't mean we should assume our students have done the same. When I asked my class to brainstorm reasons why we should read, they generated a number of generic reasons ("We'll get better grades"; "We'll get smarter"). They were able to answer the question on a superficial level, but their reasons did not really resonate with them. They were responding with the kind of generic, shallow answers they sometimes try to get away with. They answered willingly, but their responses, rote and on autopilot, were done without any real thinking. They agreed that reading was good for them, but it was obvious to me that the personal, meaningful connections were missing. They didn't really see why reading would benefit them.

This distinction between being *told* reading is good for you and being *shown* reading is good for you is an important one. To clarify this distinction, let's look at a different problem: teenage smoking. For years, teenagers have been told that smoking is bad for them. Is there a teenager in the United States who does not know this? Yet I suspect that simply telling teenagers that smoking is bad for them and that they shouldn't do it will have little or no effect. Why? Although teenagers know in a generic sense that smoking is harmful, they may not have made that connection personally. They may not have truly internalized it. The consequences of smoking might feel so distant that they have not really bought into the connection.

You might have a better chance of persuading them never to smoke if you explain the out-of-pocket additional expenses they would need to pay for car, life, and medical insurance. Maybe they would be influenced by a face-to-face meeting with emphysema victims in a cancer ward. In other words, if the negative effects of smoking could be concretely and specifically demonstrated to individual teenagers, if the consequences could be made real and immediate, my guess is you might stand a better chance to persuade them. Don't just tell them smoking is harmful; show them, and show them on a very personal level.

Much like the smoking example, simply telling students that reading is good for them will probably have little impact. We should recognize the difference between telling students that reading is good for them and showing them specifically and concretely when, where, why, and how reading will enrich their lives. Many of our students are too far removed from the real consequences of living aliterate lives (other than realizing that their grades may suffer, which in itself is not enough motivation for some). They lack the perspective to see the long-term consequences beyond the walls of the junior or senior high school classroom. We teachers will be more effective in developing readers if we broaden students' vision by personalizing reasons to read in meaningful contexts.

Attempting to show students the benefits of reading raises key questions: How do we, as adult readers, look at the world of reading from an adolescent's point of view? How do we develop reading reason lenses that will allow our students to see personal and meaningful reading reasons? Where can we find these reading reasons?

Developing a Poet's Sensibility

Before we can help our students, we must recognize that we are surrounded daily by reasons to read, so much so that we do not often see them. We have to decide consciously to be on the lookout for these reasons—to develop a reading reason lens when we interact with the world. To do this, we might think about emulating poets, who are experts at seeing things that most of us miss in everyday life. In one of my favorite poems, "Design," Robert Frost demonstrates this ability to see beyond what is in front of us:

I found a dimpled spider, fat and white,
On a white heal-all, holding up a moth
Like a white piece of rigid satin cloth—
Assorted characters of death and blight
Mixed read to begin the morning right,
Like the ingredients of a witches' broth—
A snow-drop spider, a flower like a froth,
And dead wings carried like a paper kite.

What had that flower to do with being white,
The wayside blue and innocent heal-all?
What brought the kindred spider to that height,
Then steered the white moth thither in the night?
What but design of darkness to appall?—
If design govern in a thing so small?

In all probability, if I were to come across a white spider on a white leaf holding a white moth wing, I imagine I would pause, examine it, and think, "That's pretty cool!" I might tell someone what I saw and be on my way.

Frost saw a white spider on a white leaf holding a white moth wing and his mind began to wonder whether a greater design was involved. This occurrence could not have happened randomly, he reasoned. Surely there was a grander force at work, someone or something that "steered" this design. This spider on this leaf on that day inspired Frost to metaphysically "see" much more than an insect on a flower. He used this moment as a springboard to question our place in this grand design in which we live. Frost's keen perception raises questions about the nature of fate versus free will. His poet's sensibility allowed him to dig under the surface, to consider a common experience uncommonly.

In collecting reasons to read for our students, maybe we need to develop a poet's sensibility to see below the surface. When we read a newspaper article about the average cost of raising a child, for example, this becomes more than an interesting statistic. It becomes a reason to read (raising children is expensive; reading well is financially rewarding). When I come across a magazine story about a disadvantaged, inner-city youth who rose out of the projects to become one of this nation's leading neurosurgeons, I see a reading reason (reading opens the door to college and beyond). Like Frost, who saw beyond the spider, we must see beyond the everyday items we read to make these reading connections. To do this requires a reading reason lens.

Reasons to read are everywhere. Yesterday I attended a seven-hour rules clinic to become certified as a fast-pitch softball umpire. I spent the day reading the rulebook. It looks like I'll be spending a lot of days reading the rulebook, because it contains rules like the one below. It's long and boring, and I challenge you to read it in its entirety:

Section 3. Designated Player

A.   A designated player (DP) may be used for any player provided it is made known prior to the start of the game and the player's name is indicated on the lineup as one of the nine hitters in the batting order.

B.   The name of the player for whom the DP is batting (DEFO) will be placed in the 10th position in the lineup.

C.   The starting player listed as the DP must remain in the same position in the batting order for the entire game. The DP and the DP's substitute, or the substitute's replacement, may never play offense at the same time.

D.   The DP may be substituted for at any time, either by a pinch-hitter, pinch-runner, or the DEFO. If the starting DP is replaced on offense by the DEFO, the DP will leave the game. If replaced by a substitute the DP position remains in the lineup. A starting DP may re-enter one time, as long as the DP returns to the original position in the batting order.

    1.   If replaced by the DEFO, this reduces the number of players from 10 to nine. If the DP does not re-enter, the game may legally end with nine players.

    2.   If the DP re-enters and the DEFO was batting in the DP's spot, the DEFO can return to the number 10 position and play defense only or leave the game.

E.   The DP may play defense at any position. Should the DP play defense for a player other than the one for whom the DP is batting (DEFO), that player will continue to bat but not play defense, and is not considered to have left the game. The DP may play defense for the DEFO and the DEFO is considered to have left the game, reducing the number of players from 10 to nine.

F.   The person being batted for (DEFO) may be substituted for at any time, either by a legal substitute or the DP for whom he is playing defense. The DEFO may re-enter the game one time, either in the number 10 position or in the DP's position in the batting order.

    1.   If returning to the number 10 position, the DEFO will again play defense only but may play any defensive position.

    2.   If the DEFO returns to the DP's position, the DEFO will play offense and defense; there will be only nine players in the batting order.

G.   Placing the DEFO into one of the first nine positions for someone other than the original DP is considered an illegal player and shall be disqualified. (See rule 4-7 for additional penalties.) The DEFO replacing the DP is not a substitution.

This is just one rule! When I first read it, I thought maybe I should stick to easier tasks, like solving the Israeli-Palestinian conflict, clarifying how cold fusion works, or explaining the plot of *Mullholland Drive*. My second thought, sitting in a room with three hundred other umpires, was that this rule serves as another reading reason (reading is hard, and "hard" is necessary). In this day and age, umpires who do not thoroughly know the rules run the risk of being eaten alive by coaches and parents. I will have to buckle down and study this rule in order to protect my hide. (If you think I'm being melodramatic, I invite you to come watch how some of the parents of eight-year-old girls react to their daughters being called out.) Becoming an umpire has forced me to confront difficult text—in this case, the softball rulebook. This rule is tedious, but in taking on the struggle of reading and comprehending it, I am toughening myself as a reader. By painstakingly breaking this complex rule into parts I can comprehend, I like to think I will be a bit more capable when I have to read subsequent rules. It's a bit like the weight lifter who lifts 100 pounds today so he'll be able to lift 105 pounds tomorrow.

Finding Reading Reasons Outside the Standard Curriculum

When my student Richard asked me in the library why he should read, he changed my course as a teacher. Richard taught me a number of lessons. He made me realize that many of my students are unaware of all the reasons why people like us enjoy reading, and that we, as teachers, often bury these reasons in the rush to cover the curriculum. Sure, I want kids to know the parts of speech, to be able to recognize symbolism in the novel, and to write a persuasive essay, but maybe more important, I want my students to see themselves as readers. I want them to recognize and internalize the richness the printed page will bring to their lives. Richard taught me that it's absolutely necessary to make room for these reading reasons in my already-crowded curriculum. I don't want a student to graduate from high school who can tell me what an adjective is but who will never pick up a book. To prevent this from occurring, I have to occasionally detour from the standard curriculum to sell my students on the virtues of becoming readers. The teaching of reading is the ultimate sales job.

When we make this sales pitch to students, we should get outside our comfort zones and move students into other domains of reading as well. Most states have reading standards outlining the types of reading students should be doing. The *Reading/Language Arts Framework for California Public Schools,* for example, tells teachers that students should be proficient in reading the following:

- narrative and expository text
- nonfiction
- poetry
- magazines
- newspapers
- online information

- instructional manuals
- consumer, workplace, and public documents
- political speeches
- policy statements
- platforms
- primary source documents

Many states have similar lists, which may prompt early thoughts of retirement in teachers who already feel there is not enough time in the school year to teach the curriculum. But shouldn't we consider the idea that most of the reading our students will do after graduation will not be *Macbeth* or the biology textbook? This is not a call to abandon the traditional curriculum. Rather, we need to see the value in supplementing the curriculum in each content area with related functional and "real world" reading. If my students were reading *To Kill a Mockingbird*, for example, it would help them also to read related maps, graphs, charts, magazine articles, and primary source documents to ensure they receive an enriched reading experience (see Appendix J for the Magazine Check-Out form). As writer and educator Kenneth Burke has noted, "Reading should be an imaginative rehearsal for living" (p. 29). The mini-lessons in Chapter 3 are designed to give our students as much rehearsal for the real world as possible—rehearsal for a world they will one day inherit.

The Study of "Great Things" Leads to the Discovery of a New Reading Reason

In *The Courage to Teach*, Parker Palmer argues that each discipline consists of "great things," and it should be the greatness of our subject matter that commands the attention in our classrooms. For example, in a math class Palmer suggests that "our primary responsibility as mathematicians is not to students but to mathematics; to preserve, create, and enhance good mathematics and to protect the subject for future generations" (p. 119). Parker does not favor a teacher-centered classroom or a student-centered classroom; he is proposing a *subject-centered classroom*—a place where "great things" take center stage. He writes,

> Having seen the possibility of a subject-centered classroom, I now listen anew to students' stories about their great teachers in which "a passion for the subject" is a trait so often named (a passion that need not be noisy but can be quietly intense). I always thought that passion made a great teacher because it brought contagious energy into the classroom, but now I realize its deeper function. Passion for the subject propels that subject, not the teacher, into the center of the learning circle—and when a great thing is in their midst, students have direct access to the energy of learning and life. (p. 120)

Palmer reminds me that literature is a "great thing" and that I am at my best as a teacher when I step aside and allow the greatness of literature to be the center of my classroom. After all, whose intellect should be front and center in the classroom? The intellect of Shakespeare, Joyce, and Homer, or the intellect of Kelly Gallagher? This is also a reminder that I do not need to trivialize the greatness of literature by having students present a mock Jerry Springer skit with Miss Havisham as a guest. Or by having students spend valuable class time outlining Tom Robinson's trial in their classroom edition of the *Maycomb News*. Gimmicks are unnecessary when the depth of great literature beckons. The big ideas, the ethical and moral dilemmas present in a great work, should be the center of attention for students and teachers alike.

As I write this, my eldest daughter, a ninth grader, has just finished reading a "great thing" in her English class—*Romeo and Juliet*. Her teacher has assigned the following essay question:

> At the end of the play, the Prince announces, "Some shall be pardoned, and some punished." Write an essay that argues who should be punished and who should be pardoned. Cite specific examples from the play to support your position.

Watching my daughter struggle with this question makes me appreciate the value of reading Shakespeare, and that this value goes far beyond acquiring what E. D. Hirsch terms "cultural literacy." The real value lies in her examination of the characters' motives and behavior. Exploring the ethical dilemmas the characters face and the choices they make requires her to wrestle with our humanness, our morality. In reading *Romeo and Juliet*, she is confronted by the following questions:

- Does violence solve problems?
- Can long-term feuds ever be buried?
- Are there times when secrets should be told?
- Is teenage love real love?
- Is love at first sight possible?
- Can love blind you to reason?
- How much say should parents have regarding whom their children date?
- Do you pilot your own life, or is there a greater force involved?
- Is there such thing as good luck? bad luck?
- Is suicide ever a reasonable option?

As these questions illustrate, there is a reason why people have been reading *Romeo and Juliet* for over four hundred years, and it's not just because it's a romance (otherwise, we might as well have students read the *Sweet Valley High* series instead). *Romeo and Juliet* is a "great thing." This play's popularity has endured because the questions it raises are important, and they are as relevant today as they were in 1594. The issues raised in this play speak to the universality of the human condition.

In the next four years, my daughter will read many great books in her English classes. In doing so she will explore racism through the eyes of Atticus Finch, search to find her identity through the travails of Pip and Holden Caufield, and consider human nature by judging the actions of Ralph, Piggy, and Jack. She'll look at persecution through the eyes of Hester Prynne, think about the effects of materialism, ambition, and greed by studying Jay Gatsby, and see firsthand the disastrous effects of lust from Hamlet's perspective.

But big ideas are certainly not limited to the literature found in her English classes. In other content-area classes, I like to believe she'll read the thoughts of Cesar Chavez, Albert Einstein, Abraham Lincoln, Steven Hawking, Gandhi, Martin Luther King Jr., and others. If handled with serious respect and scholarship, this reading journey she will soon travel will provide her with an ethical practice training ground. By presenting her with imaginative rehearsals for living, these reading experiences will better equip her to manage the challenges of adulthood.

It was while watching my daughter struggle with the *Romeo and Juliet* essay question that I began to see the emergence of a new reading reason.

A Tenth Reading Reason Emerges

The reading journey my daughter is embarking on brings to mind the story of *Gilgamesh,* believed to be over five thousand years old. Reading it, I am struck by how little humans have changed over the course of time. *Gilgamesh,* which was etched into clay tablets, is essentially a story about the importance of friendship and loyalty, of coping with loss and grief, of confronting our mortality.

Though the world we live in today is drastically different, reading *Gilgamesh* underscores the idea that though the world has changed, the people living in this world haven't changed much at all. What concerned people five thousand years ago still concerns us today; what concerns us today will concern others five thousand years from now. This reminds me of Virginia Woolf, who once said, "Literature is no one's private ground, literature is common ground; let us trespass freely and fearlessly and find our way for ourselves." I like the paradox of that statement: to find our individuality, we must explore common ground. In this case, the reading of great things provides that common ground. As Descartes said, "The reading of all great books is like conversation with the finest men of past centuries." When our students read *Gilgamesh,* or Carl Sagan's *Cosmos,* or the Declaration of Independence, or Martin Luther King Jr.'s *Letter from a Birmingham Jail,* or other great works, they are finding their way for themselves by joining the human conversation.

While I believe strongly that the reading of classic works serves as an ethical training ground, this moral development can also be reaped from reading other sources as well. For example, in a single edition of the *Los Angeles Times,* the following moral questions are asked outright or implied:

- What plan would offer the best prospects for peace in the Middle East?
- Should the United States take a more active role in the Palestinian-Israeli conflict?
- Is suicide bombing an act of bravery or cowardice?
- How long should the war in Afghanistan continue?
- What should the punishment be for those responsible for the Enron debacle?
- Why can so few afford to purchase a home?
- Should we be developing genetic food?
- Should Cardinal Roger Mahoney of the Los Angeles archdiocese release the names of all priests accused of sexual misconduct?
- Are enough underrepresented students gaining admission to our best universities?
- Should sheriff's deputies be able to use "reasonable force" to obtain DNA samples from inmates?
- Do the bus drivers of the Los Angeles Unified School District have just cause in going out on strike this week?
- Will the recent legislation mandating campaign finance reform prove to be effective?
- Should obese people be able to deduct out-of-pocket expenses from their taxes for weight-loss efforts?
- Should the state of California honor the contracts it signed with providers of electrical power?
- Will the Dodgers win a game this year? (Okay, this isn't a moral question, but the boys in blue are 0–3 and things aren't looking good.)

Some of these questions are more important than others, and by the time you read this you may know many of the answers; my point is that reading the newspaper, much like reading a classic work, provides an opportunity for us to develop our morality. The issues raised by the questions above appeared in a single edition of the newspaper. Tomorrow there will be counterpoint to some of the opinions expressed in this edition, and this counterpoint will, no doubt, expand readers' thinking on these issues. Our moral development, and the moral growth of our students, will develop naturally if we read the newspaper regularly. Beyond the newspaper, this development continues when our students read materials about science, history, art, politics, religion, philosophy, and other subjects.

Development of our moral compass never ends. Even as adults, we are constantly fine-tuning it whenever we read a book, watch a provocative film, or peruse a thoughtful magazine. When reading, what are we most drawn to? Where is our attention generally focused? I would make the case that we are drawn to human conflict as we read. Fiction or nonfiction, it is the conflict people are involved in that captures our attention. (Think of a film or book that bored you. Chances are that you did not connect to the conflict found in that work.) It is the consideration of conflicts that makes us think, that challenges us to consider where we stand, and that shapes our moral development as human beings.

So, after writing a book that proposes nine reasons to read I am led to the discovery of a tenth reason: Reading develops our moral compass. When I am successful in getting my students to see the relevance that books play in their lives, lightbulbs go on and magic occurs. Students see themselves in great works. When I am unsuccessful in getting students to see the relevance, drudgery occurs. If my students cannot make moral connections between great books and their own lives, they are doing nothing more than reading stories. Great writing matters, and by examining great works, teachers and students are provided rich opportunities to wrestle with universal ethical and moral dilemmas—the same dilemmas faced by humans centuries ago, and the same dilemmas our great-grandchildren will face.

The idea that great writing develops our moral compass has been in my mind ever since I began teaching literature. Like most English teachers, I spend time discussing themes and universal truths with students. But it wasn't until I sat down to write this chapter that I considered sharing this idea with students as another reason to read. Thus, the writing of this chapter has led me to add a tenth reason to the list of reading reasons:

1. Reading is rewarding.
2. Reading builds a mature vocabulary.
3. Reading makes you a better writer.
4. Reading is hard, and "hard" is necessary.
5. Reading makes you smarter.
6. Reading prepares you for the world of work.
7. Reading well is financially rewarding.
8. Reading opens the door to college and beyond.
9. Reading arms you against oppression.
10. Reading develops your moral compass.

Are there other reasons to read? Certainly. By the time you read this, my reading reasons list may have thirteen or fourteen reasons on it. I'm sure many of you, while reading this book, thought of your own reasons—ones that have not occurred to me. Developing reasons and lessons is an ongoing process, organically grown from our reading experiences and our unique, daily interaction with adolescents.

Riding a Dead Horse

In *If You're Riding a Horse and It Dies, Get Off,* Jim Grant and Char Forsten have written a biting satire on the state of our school system. They note that if the horse you're riding is, indeed, dead, you will not ride faster if you use a bigger whip, or change riders, or have a committee examine the animal. Blaming the horse's parents or raising the standards for riding will not help, either. If the horse you are riding is truly dead, there is only one course of action: get off the horse and ride something new.

Sometimes I think we are still riding the same reading horse. We are still putting reluctant readers on computer reading programs. We are still giving students lots of exercises and reading quizzes. We are still blaming the students' parents. These approaches are not working. If you buy into the idea that adolescents are reading less than they did ten or twenty years ago and that the trend is getting worse rather than better, maybe our approach to adolescent readers is not working. We have all heard the expression "If it ain't broke, don't fix it." We need to consider the flip side of this expression: "If it ain't working, change it." It's time to mount a new horse.

The reading reasons found in this book were born out of the realization that if I want my students to become lifelong readers, then I, as their teacher, need to do something different. As someone once said, "If you always do what you've always done, you'll always get what you've always got." I have come to the realization that I can't continue doing business as usual with my students. The traditional reading approach—simply telling them that reading is good for them—has little effect in lighting their reading fires. They have become numb to this message. My students, like yours, want to see, want to feel, want to know what's in it for them. The reading reasons in this book address the reading problem by showing students the rewards reading will offer them. These reasons have resonated with my students, and I trust they will with yours as well.

I'll end with the first words of this book. Donald Graves said, "If you make a student feel like a reader, he'll become a reader." Showing students why they should read is the first and most important step in this process.

APPENDIXES

Appendix A: The Three Commandments of Developing a Classroom Library
Appendix B: 101 Books Every Classroom Library Should Have
Appendix C: Monthly Bulletin Board Ideas to Promote Reading
Appendix D: Book Donation Label
Appendix E: Books Recommended by Students Form
Appendix F: Parent Classroom Library Letter
Appendix G: Books Read by the Magnolia High School Faculty Book Club
Appendix H: Reading Log
Appendix I: Reading Record
Appendix J: Magazine Check-Out
Appendix K: Classroom Time Chart

Appendix A

The Three Commandments of Developing a Classroom Library

Appendix B lists 101 books every junior and senior high school classroom should have. When considering the titles on these lists, thou shalt keep in mind the Three Commandments of Classroom Libraries.

Commandment 1: Thou Shalt Realize That Appropriateness Is Relative

Walk into a public library, find the adolescent literature section, put on a blindfold, and select one book at random. I can guarantee you that there is a parent out there who will object to that book, regardless of what title you have chosen. Parents' views about what their children can read vary widely, and as teachers, we need to be sensitive to this. One parent of an eighth grader might encourage her son to read Stephen King, while another might call the school to complain when Junior comes home with *It* from your classroom library.

For example, one year I taught seniors first period and freshmen second period. This required a rather drastic cognitive shift in my brain between 9:00 and 9:05 A.M. It was almost like teaching at two different schools (or, at times, like two different planets!). As a result, my classroom library, which consists of 2,500 books, has a wide range of "appropriateness." There are books on my shelves that I want seniors to read that may not be appropriate for some of my freshmen. In essence, my classroom is no different than a public library.

In order to avoid problems with parents, I send a letter home with the students explaining the concept of a classroom library (see Appendix F). Students must receive permission from their parents to gain access to the classroom library—sort of a classroom library card, if you will. I explain to parents that my classroom library, like any library, has a range of appropriateness, and that, as parents, they should be aware of what their children are reading. I also have parents sign their students' reading log weekly. These precautionary moves head off most problems.

Commandment 2: Thou Shalt Recognize That Classroom Library Book Loss Is Unavoidable and Is Sometimes a Good Thing

If you have interesting books, kids will read them. If you have interesting books, you will lose some of them. There are a lot of worse things that can happen to teachers than students taking books and wanting to keep them.

However, let's be realistic. I do not know a single teacher who is independently wealthy, so we must take steps to stem our losses of good books.

Here are some suggestions to keep your classroom library well stocked at relatively little or no cost:

- Create a checkout system, preferably student-operated, to track your books. When students check out a book from my library, they take a small index card and write their name, the name of the book, and the date on the card. They do not give me the card; rather, each period has a designated "book administrator" (a teacher-aide or reliable student). I have enough to do without chasing books all day. The book administrator files the card in a card box alphabetically. Every two weeks the cards are pulled and the administrator checks to see who still has books out, whether they are still reading them, and who will be returning books soon. The book administrator also manages waiting lists for specific books. Some teachers in my school district use handheld pen bar code readers as a way of tracking their classroom library books.
- Create a stamp to identify your books. I had a stamp made at a stationery store that reads, "Please return this book to Mr. Gallagher, room 7, Magnolia High School." I stamp the title page and the side of the pages of each book. This $10 investment has paid off many times by the number of lost books that are returned to me every year.
- Conduct a once-a-year book drive to replenish your library. Make it a competition between classes.
- Ask students to identify their favorite books and donate them. I have every graduating senior donate a book before leaving the school. I ask them to choose the books they most enjoyed reading in high school. I created a sticker that includes the school's insignia and room for students to write their name and a brief personal message (see Appendix D). Students like the idea of leaving a little bit of their reading legacies behind for future students to enjoy. Though I do this with seniors, it could certainly be done at any grade level.
- Write local businesses, explaining your need for books. One local business I contacted ran an employee book drive that netted 500 books for my school.
- Contact your local library and ask if they ever sell books. Twice a year my local library has a "blow-out" sale where one can purchase four books for $1. Garage sales are a good source as well, as are local Goodwill and Salvation Army stores.
- Earn credit toward books by having students participate in book clubs. My students purchase books monthly from Scholastic, which offers high-interest reading titles at reasonable prices. For every dollar my students spend, I earn one point, which goes toward free books at the end of the year. For information on the Scholastic program, call 1-800-724-6527 or contact them on the Web at Scholastic.com.
- Ask your doctor and dentist to keep old magazines for you. Stop by once a month and pick them up.

Commandment 3: Thou Shalt Understand That in a Classroom Library, Books Need to Be Marketed

Jim Trelease is right when he says that we can all learn from the way Barnes and Noble markets their books inside their stores. Their sales pitch is evident from the moment you walk in the door. Their books are on display, nicely lit, with the covers, not the spines, facing you. In every one of their sections—new fiction, staff recommendations, best-sellers—the books are facing you, enticing you to browse.

Does the displaying of books really make a difference? At the Lafayette Public Library in Colorado, librarians conducted their own experiment. They purchased two copies of each of 182 adult fiction titles and 398 nonfiction titles. All books purchased were at least a year old. For each title, one of the copies was displayed and the other one was shelved. The library had a check-out period of three weeks, with a single renewal of an additional three weeks. The results? "Of the 182 fiction titles, display copies were checked out 348 times, compared to 180 times for shelf copies. That is an increase of 96 percent for display copies. Of the 398 nonfiction titles, 382 display copies were checked out, compared to 306 shelf copies. That is an increase of 25 percent for display copies." Simply displaying the books raised the circulation significantly.

If we want to entice our students to read, we must display our classroom library books. Here are some marketing ideas:

- Hang heavy-duty wire clotheslines across your room above the heads of the students. Using wooden clothespins, hang your best books so they are "floating" just above your students throughout your classroom.
- Purchase inexpensive plastic rain gutters from a hardware store. Affix them to the walls of your classroom and set books in them so the covers can be seen.
- Once a week, line five or six books, face out, on your chalk trays. Pick them thematically and give brief book talks.
- Prior to class, place one interesting book on every student's desk. Pick a wide range of genres. Have students read each book for two minutes, then rotate the books.

Keeping these three commandments in mind will increase the effectiveness of your classroom library.

Appendix B

101 Books Every Classroom Library Should Have

101 Books for Junior High

Coming of Age/Peer Pressure/Relationships

1. *Because of Winn-Dixie,* Kate DiCamillo. Ten-year-old Opal learns family secrets after moving to a small town in Florida.
2. *Bridge to Terabithia,* Katherine Paterson. The story of a great friendship between Jess and Leslie, both fifth-grade outcasts.
3. *Dogland,* Will Shetterly. Set against the backdrop of the civil rights movement, this is a story of a family who moves to Florida to open an unusual tourist attraction.
4. *Dove and Sword: A Novel of Joan of Arc,* Nancy Garden. The tale of Gabrielle, a fictional close friend of Joan of Arc.
5. *Everything on a Waffle,* Polly Horvath. Primrose, who fails to believe her parents are really lost at sea, hangs out with many interesting characters at the local café.
6. *Freak the Mighty,* Rodman Philbrick. Maxwell, who is unusually large for his age, strikes up an unconventional friendship with Kevin, whose growth is stunted by a birth defect.
7. *From the Mixed-Up Files of Mrs. Basil E. Frankweiler,* E. L. Konigsburg. Claudia, twelve, and Jamie, eight, run away from home and hide in New York's Metropolitan Museum of Art.
8. *Holes,* Louis Sachar. Stanley, though innocent, is sent to a boys' detention camp to dig daily holes in the hot sun. Once there, he makes an interesting discovery.
9. *Hush,* Jacqueline Woodson. After her father witnesses a brutal crime, Toswiah and her family are sent into the witness protection program.
10. *Jacob Have I Loved,* Katherine Peterson. Louise, a young girl in a small fishing town, struggles to emerge from the shadow of her beautiful and talented twin sister.
11. *The Land,* Mildred Taylor. A prequel to *Roll of Thunder, Hear My Cry,* this book chronicles how the Logan family came to Mississippi.
12. *Lemony Snicket: A Series of Unfortunate Events* (series), Lemony Snicket. Fans of Harry Potter will love this darker series about three orphans and their adventures.
13. *A Long Way from Chicago: A Novel in Stories,* Richard Peck. Joey and Mary Alice are sent to their grandmother's country home for their formative years. Each chapter chronicles a different year.
14. *Make Lemonade,* Virginia Euwer Wolff. The story of a fourteen-year-old girl's struggle to escape poverty through education.
15. *Maniac Magee,* Jerry Spinelli. A folktale of a young boy who confronts racism and a whole lot more.

16. *The Misfits,* James Howe. Four middle school misfits, tired of the teasing, take action.

17. *Nightjohn,* Gary Paulsen. A story of slavery on a southern plantation. Nightjohn risks his life to educate others.

18. *The Night of the Twisters,* Ivy Ruckman. Two boys struggle for survival when a killer tornado levels their town.

19. *Nothing but the Truth,* Avi. A freshman's run-in with his English teacher draws national attention.

20. *The Princess Diaries,* Meg Cabot. Mia is a typical ninth grader until she discovers she has become the crowned princess of a small country.

21. *Raptor Red,* Robert Bakker. An account of what it might have been like to be a dinosaur 120 million years ago.

22. *Rules of the Road,* Joan Bauer. Jenna, a sophomore, learns lessons about life as she drives across the country.

23. *The Runaways,* Zilpha Keatley Snyder. After her family moves from the coast to the desert, Dani's plans to run away lead her to adventures.

24. *Shabanu, Daughter of the Wind,* Maureen Fisher Staples. The story of a strong-willed eleven-year-old girl raised in a close-knit family of nomadic sheepherders in the deserts of Pakistan.

25. *Shadow Spinner,* Susan Fletcher. Marjan, an orphan, is forced by the prince to be the discoverer of new stories.

26. *Shiloh,* Phyllis Naylor. An eleven-year-old is faced with some difficult decisions when he finds an abused dog.

27. *A Single Shard,* Linda Sue Park. Set in twelfth-century Korea, this is the story of an orphan boy raised to be a master potter.

28. *Skellig,* David Almond. Upon moving into a new house, Michael uncovers a strange and mysterious discovery in the garage.

29. *Sparrow Hawk Red,* Ben Mikaelsen. Ricky tries to avenge the death of his mother, who was mistakenly killed by drug lords.

30. *Speak,* Laurie Halse Anderson. Melinda, a high school freshman, is reluctant to talk to anyone after something terrible happens to her.

31. *The Starplace,* Vicky Grove. The story of Celeste, the first black student to attend the white junior high school in Quiver, Oklahoma, in 1961.

32. *Stepping on the Cracks,* Mary Downing Hahn. Two girls discover a conscientious objector hiding from the World War II battlefield.

33. *Stuck in Neutral,* Terry Trueman. The story of a teenager trapped inside of his own body due to cerebral palsy.

34. *Tangerine,* Edward Bloor. Paul, a vision-impaired seventh grader, moves to a new school and has some epiphanies about his family's past.

35. *The Tiger Rising,* Kate Dicamillo. A young boy finds a caged tiger in the woods behind a motel. This discovery leads to many others.

36. *A Time for Dancing,* Davida Hills Hurwin. The lives of two high school friends are shattered when one of them is diagnosed with cancer.

37. *Touching Spirit Bear,* Ben Mikaelsen. Cole, a defiant ninth grader, is banished for one year to a remote Alaskan island.

38. *Walk Two Moons,* Sharon Creech. A thirteen-year-old travels with her grandparents in search of her mother's history.

39. *The Wanderer,* Sharon Creech. Thirteen-year-old Sophie takes a perilous cross-Atlantic journey.

40. *The Watsons Go to Birmingham—1963,* Christopher Paul Curtis. A fictional account of an African-American family's journey in the violent summer of 1963.

41. *When Zachary Beaver Came to Town,* Kimberly Willis Holt. The world's fattest boy comes to a small Texas town and prompts young Toby to discover some humanity.

42. *A Year Down Yonder,* Richard Peck. The Newberry Medal–winning sequel to *A Long Way from Chicago.*

Adventure

43. *Earthquake at Dawn,* Kristina Gregory. A historical fictional account of the earthquake that rocked San Francisco in 1906.

44. *October Sky,* Homer Hickman. Homer, inspired to leave the coal mines of West Virginia, decides at the age of fourteen to build a rocket. Little did he know where this journey would take him.

45. *The Perfect Storm,* Sebastian Junger. The true story of the fishermen aboard the *Andrea Gail,* who were caught at sea in the storm of the century.

Sports

46. *Danger Zone,* David Klass. A story of basketball and racism as told through the eyes of Jimmy Doyle, teenage basketball star.

47. *Heaven Is a Playground,* Rick Telander. A book that chronicles the passions involved in inner-city playground basketball.

48. *Ironman,* Chris Crutcher. Bo, who was thrown off the high school football team, trains for a triathlon as a way of coping with his anger.

49. *It's Not About the Bike,* Lance Armstrong. Is there a more inspirational athlete in the world than Lance Armstrong?

50. *The Moves Make the Man,* Bruce Brooks. A friendship develops through two boys' love of the game of basketball.

Nonfiction

51. *Chicken Soup for the Soul* (series). Inspirational stories for all interests, from pet lovers to baseball fans.

52. *Gifted Hands: The Ben Carson Story,* Ben Carson. The true story of a boy who rose from the projects to become one of the leading neurosurgeons in the world.

53. *Listening with My Heart,* Heather Whitestone. The story of Heather Whitestone, the first Miss America with a physical disability.

54. *One Child,* Torey Hayden. A teacher's fight to save an abused, brilliant student.

55. *Portraits of Grief, New York Times.* A collection of vignettes on the people who lost their lives in the World Trade Center attack.

56. *Red Scarf Girl: A Memoir of the Cultural Revolution,* Ji-Li Jiang. A compelling memoir of a girl's gradual disillusionment with communism.

57. *Tuesdays with Morrie,* Mitch Albon. A young man chronicles his visits to his dying friend and mentor.

58. *Warriors Don't Cry: A Searing Memoir of the Battle to Integrate Little Rock's Central High,* Melba Pattilo Beals. The story of the Little Rock Nine, who risked their lives to go to school.
59. *We Were There, Too: Young People in U.S. History,* Phillip Hoose. Vignettes of young people who witnessed U.S. history firsthand.
60. *The Worst-Case Scenario Survival Handbook,* David Borgenicht. Would you know what to do if you found yourself stuck in quicksand?

Mystery

61. *Boy's Life,* Robert McCammon. A young boy's life is forever changed after he witnesses the disposal of a murder victim.
62. *Face on a Milk Carton,* Caroline Cooney. Fifteen-year-old Janie Johnson recognizes herself in a picture of a kidnapped three-year-old on a milk carton.
63. *Ghost Canoe,* Will Hobbs. Part adventure story, part mystery, part historical fiction.
64. *Harry Potter* (series), J. K. Rowling. No blurb necessary.
65. *Hush, Little Baby,* Caroline Cooney. Kit finds a baby wrapped in a bundle and is unaware that this will put her in danger.
66. *Monster,* Walter Dean Myers. The story of a teenager arrested for murder during a botched robbery. But did he really do it?

Fantasy/Science Fiction

67. *Among the Hidden,* Margaret Peterson Haddix. Luke is the third child in a society where family size is severely restricted to two children. He meets others who plan a rebellion.
68. *The Angel Factory,* Terence Blacker. A twelve-year-old-boy hacks into a computer and discovers a family secret and worldwide conspiracy in this futuristic thriller.
69. *The Dragonriders of Pern* (series), Anne McCaffrey. An imaginative adventure-fantasy series.
70. *The Egypt Game,* Zilpha Kathy Snyder. When a group of children are introduced to the Egypt Game, little do they know it will lead to a murder mystery.
71. *The Giver,* Lois Lowry. In this futuristic story, Jonas is one of the chosen few who have the ability to remember the past.
72. *The Haunting of Holroyd Hill,* Brenda Seabrooke. Part love story, ghost story, mystery, and historical fiction (Civil War).
73. *His Dark Materials* (trilogy): *The Golden Compass, The Subtle Knife,* and *The Amber Spyglass,* Philip Pullman. Fans of Harry Potter will like this series.
74. *The Last of the Really Great Whangdoodles,* Julie Andrews Edwards. Three children visit a magical land filled with comical creatures.
75. *The Phantom Tollbooth,* Norman Juster. A ten-year-old boy discovers a large toy tollbooth in his bedroom that allows him to undertake a remarkable journey.
76. *The Root Cellar,* Janet Louise Swoboda Lunn. Rose, twelve, discovers a secret passageway in the root cellar that allows her to climb into another century.
77. *Running Out of Time,* Margaret Peterson Haddix. Jessie, a thirteen-year-old girl, lives in the 1840s. Or does she?

78. *Sandry's Book (Circle of Magic 1),* Tamora Pierce. Sandry and her magical friends use their powers when confronted by disaster.
79. *The Westing Game,* Ellen Raskin. A millionaire is murdered and there are many heirs. Who did it?
80. *Tuck Everlasting,* Natalie Babbitt. The Tuck family is blessed (or is it cursed?) with the discovery of eternal life.
81. *Wise Child,* Monica Furlong. A blend of fantasy and historical fiction, this is the story of a young girl raised to be a good witch in a twelfth-century Scottish village.

Humor

82. *And I Thought I Was Crazy! Quirks, Idiosyncrasies and Meshugas,* Judy Reiser. Do you turn all your coat hangers the same way?
83. *Duh! The Stupid History of the Human Race,* Bob Fenster. After reading this, you'll wonder how our species has survived.
84. *The Far Side* (cartoon series), Gary Larson. A classroom favorite.
85. *Letters from a Nut,* Ted L. Nancy. Hilarious letters written to actual companies and the responses they elicit.
86. *Presumed Ignorant,* Leland Gregory. Did you know that in Santa Ana, California, it is illegal to swim on dry land? These and other goofy laws still on the books are found here.
87. *What's the Number for 911?,* Leland Gregory. Strange but true 911 calls.
88. *You May Not Tie an Alligator to a Fire Hydrant: 101 Real Dumb Laws,* Jeff Koon. Did you know it's illegal to leave a gate open in Nevada?

Poetry

89. *Amber Was Brave, Essie Was Smart,* Vera Williams. The story of two young sisters in a struggling family told through a series of poems.
90. *A Box of Rain,* Abigail Lynne Becker. An anthology of poems written by Abi Becker, who tragically lost her life in an automobile accident at the age of seventeen.
91. *Ego-Tripping and Other Poems for Young People,* Nikki Giovanni. Giovanni eloquently writes of the African-American experience.
92. *Heart to Heart: New Poems Inspired by Twentieth-Century American Art,* Jan Greenberg. Forty-eight works of art, each coupled with original poems written by well-known poets.
93. *Nineteen Varieties of Gazelle: Poems of the Middle East,* Naomi Shihab Nye. Gathered after September 11, this collection of poems captures what it is like to be an Arab living in the United States.
94. *Out of the Dust,* Karen Hesse. The dust bowl as seen through the poetry of fourteen-year-old Billie Jo.
95. *This Same Sky,* Naomi Shihab Nye. Over one hundred poets from sixty-eight countries are found in this collection.
96. *Witness,* Karen Hesse. Set in Vermont, 1924, this set of poems examines the attempts of the Ku Klux Klan to infiltrate a small town.

Holocaust

97. *All but My Life,* Gerda Weissman Klein. The memoir of a young Jewish girl's enslavement by the Nazis and the story of her liberation.

98. *The Cage,* Ruth Minsky Sender. A thirteen-year-old girl is separated from her family and sent to a concentration camp.

99. *From Ashes to Life: My Memories of the Holocaust,* Lucille Eichengreen. An unflinching Holocaust memoir.

100. *In My Hands: Memories of a Holocaust Rescuer,* Irene Gut Opdyke. The autobiography of a World War II nurse who witnessed a number of atrocities firsthand.

101. *Number the Stars,* Lois Lowry. A family's attempt to smuggle a Jewish family to safety.

101 Books for Senior High

Coming of Age/Peer Pressure/Relationships

1. *Big Mouth and Ugly Girl,* Joyce Carol Oates. Matt, a junior, gets in trouble when a comment of his is misinterpreted. Ursula, a.k.a. Ugly Girl, comes to his defense.

2. *Breaking Point,* Alex Flinn. Paul, a high school student, is harassed by other students. He has to make some tough choices if he wants to be popular.

3. *Breathing Underwater,* Alex Flinn. Nick has to face repercussions after striking his girlfriend.

4. *Buried Onions,* Gary Soto. Eddie tries to escape poverty and gangs on the poor side of Fresno, California.

5. *Chicana Falsa and Other Stories of Death, Identity, and Oxnard,* Michele Serros. A collection of poems and stories from a Chicana perspective.

6. *Crystal,* Walter Dean Myers. Through the eyes of sixteen-year-old Crystal, we see the darker side of the modeling world.

7. *Damage,* A. M. Jenkins. A high school football star struggles with depression and thoughts of suicide.

8. *Divine Secrets of the Ya-Ya Sisterhood,* Rebecca Wells. The story of Sidda Walker's estranged relationship with her mother.

9. *Feeling Sorry for Celia,* Jaclyn Moriarty. The life of a lonely fifteen-year-old Australian girl is examined through a series of letters.

10. *Hope Was Here,* Joan Bauer. Hope, sixteen, and her Aunt Addie leave the big city to work in a small town café.

11. *I'll Be Seeing You,* Lurlene McDaniel. The story of a young girl who tries to find love despite having her face disfigured by surgery.

12. *Keeping the Moon,* Sarah Dessen. Colie Sparks expects the worst when she is sent to spend the summer with her eccentric aunt.

13. *Life Is Funny,* E. R. Frank. The lives and loves of eleven Brooklyn teens are chronicled.

14. *Like Water for Chocolate,* Laura Esquivel. A love story set against the backdrop of the Mexican revolution.

15. *Love and Other Four-Letter Words,* Carolyn Mackler. Sammie, sixteen, whose parents are having a trial separation, moves to New York with her mom.

16. *Parrot in the Oven: Mi Vida,* Victor Martinez. Manuel, a Mexican-American teen, struggles with inner-city racism, poverty, and violence.

17. *Peace Like a River,* Leif Enger. Rube Land narrates the memory of events in his eleventh year, the year his brother David shot two town bullies.

18. *The Princess Diaries,* Meg Cabot. Mia is a typical ninth grader until she discovers she has become the crowned princess of a small country.

19. *Screen Test,* David Klass. Liz, a beautiful but naïve New Jersey teenager, leaves home for the summer to star in a movie in Los Angeles.

20. *Shabanu, Daughter of the Wind,* Maureen Fisher Staples. The story of a strong-willed eleven-year-old girl raised in a close-knit family of nomadic sheepherders in the deserts of Pakistan.

21. *The Sisterhood of the Traveling Pants,* Ann Brashares. It's amazing what a pair of pants will do to raise the spirits of four friends separated for the summer.

22. *Skellig,* David Almond. Upon moving into a new house, Michael uncovers a strange and mysterious discovery in the garage.

23. *So Far from God,* Ana Castillo. Three generations of Latinas are captured in this sometimes tragic, sometimes funny rip-roaring novel.

24. *Speak,* Laurie Halse Anderson. Melinda, a high school freshman, confronts the boy who raped her at last year's end-of-summer party.

25. *Swallowing Stones,* Joyce McDonald. A teenager fires a bullet into the air to celebrate his seventeenth birthday. When the bullet lands, his life is forever changed.

26. *Tenth Grade: A Novel,* Joseph Weisberg. The life of an average high school sophomore boy as told through his daily journal.

27. *True Believer,* Virginia Euwer Wolff. Verna, fifteen, must overcome the temptations of inner-city life if she is to reach her goal of attending a university.

28. *Truth or Diary,* Catherine Clark. Courtney, a high school senior in the wake of a breakup with her boyfriend, swears off boys for one year.

29. *Who Is Eddie Leonard?* Harry Mazer. Eddie, fifteen, begins to believe he is not who his parents say he is.

30. *You Don't Know Me,* David Klass. At fourteen, John feels trapped when his mother dates an abusive man.

Adventure

31. *Alive,* Piers Paul Read. An extraordinary nonfictional account of a soccer team's will to survive after crashing in the Andes Mountains.

32. *Cold Mountain,* Charles Frazier. Inman, a wounded Confederate soldier, decides he has had enough of war and begins a cross-country walk home to the woman he loves.

33. *The Day the Sky Split Apart,* Roy Gallant. A nonfictional account of the Tunguska meteorite, which struck Earth with a fireball explosion in 1908.

34. *Dove,* Robin Lee Graham. The true story of a sixteen-year-old boy who sails around the world alone.

35. *Endurance: Shackleton's Incredible Voyage,* Alfred Lansing. The true story of twenty-eight men who are trapped in Arctic ice and their heroic struggle for survival.

36. *In the Heart of the Sea: The Tragedy of the Whaleship Essex*, Nathaniel Philbrick. The story that inspired *Moby-Dick*, this is the harrowing tale of a whaling crew trying to survive after their ship is sunk.

37. *Into Thin Air*, Jon Krakauer. A firsthand, riveting account of a mountaineering disaster that took the lives of eight climbers.

38. *October Sky*, Homer Hickman. Homer, inspired to leave the coal mines of West Virginia, decides at the age of fourteen to build a rocket. Little did he know where this journey would take him.

39. *The Perfect Storm*, Sebastian Junger. The true story of the fishermen aboard the *Andrea Gail*, who were caught at sea in the storm of the century.

40. *Raptor Red*, Robert Bakker. An account of what it might have been like to be a dinosaur 120 million years ago.

41. *Ship of Gold in the Deep Blue Sea*, Gary Kinder. The true-life race to find the *Central American*, which sunk in 1857 with 600 men and millions of dollars of gold treasure on board.

True Crime

42. *The Blooding*, Joseph Wambaugh. The first time DNA is used to catch a killer, in this case a mass murderer in England.

43. *In Cold Blood*, Truman Capote. A harrowing and violent account of murder in a small town.

44. *The Killing Season: A Summer Inside an LAPD Homicide Division*, Miles Corwin. A reporter follows two homicide investigators through a hot Los Angeles summer.

45. *Who Killed My Daughter?* Lois Duncan. Duncan, who writes mysteries, is searching for the real-life killer of her eighteen-year-old daughter.

46. *Zodiac*, Robert Graysmith. An account of the grisly Zodiac killings in San Francisco.

Sports

47. *Danger Zone*. David Klass. A story of basketball and racism as told through the eyes of Jimmy Doyle, teenage basketball star.

48. *Fall River Dreams: A Team's Quest for Glory—a Town's Search for Its Soul*, Bill Reynolds. The true story of four high school basketball players with dreams of bigger things.

49. *Friday Night Lights*, H. G. Bissinger. A nonfictional account of high school football madness in a small Texas town.

50. *Heaven Is a Playground*, Rick Telander. A book that chronicles the passions involved in inner-city playground basketball.

51. *The Last Shot: City Streets, Basketball Dreams*, Darcy Frey. The chronicles of four boys in search of college basketball scholarships.

52. *The Moves Make the Man*, Bruce Brooks. A friendship develops through two boys' love of the game of basketball.

53. *Seabiscuit: An American Legend*, Laura Hillenbrand. A riveting account of the racehorse Seabiscuit, who was arguably the biggest celebrity in America in the 1930s.

Nonfiction

54. *And Still We Rise: The Trials and Triumphs of Twelve Gifted Inner-City Students,* Miles Corwin. A year-long chronicle of advanced placement students trying to overcome inner-city obstacles.
55. *Bird by Bird,* Anne Lamott. Advice about writing and life.
56. *Chicken Soup for the Soul* (series). Inspirational stories for all interests, from pet lovers to baseball fans.
57. *Fast Food Nation,* Eric Schlosser. You might not eat another hamburger again after reading this inside account of the fast food industry.
58. *The Hot Zone,* Richard Preston. A dramatic, scary account of an outbreak of the Ebola virus and health officials' struggle to contain it.
59. *Listening with My Heart,* Heather Whitestone. The story of Heather Whitestone, the first Miss America with a physical disability.
60. *The Lives of a Cell: Notes of a Biology Watcher,* Lewis Thomas. A philosophical look at the role biology plays in our lives.
61. *Tuesdays with Morrie,* Mitch Albon. A young man chronicles his visits to his dying friend and mentor.
62. *Warriors Don't Cry: A Searing Memoir of the Battle to Integrate Little Rock's Central High,* Melba Pattilo Beals. The story of the Little Rock Nine, who risked their lives to go to school.
63. *The Worst-Case Scenario Survival Handbook,* David Borgenicht. Would you know what to do if you found yourself stuck in quicksand?

Immigration/Coming to America

64. *Jasmine,* Bharati Mukherjee. Jasmine overcomes tragedy as she emigrates from India to Ohio.
65. *Red Scarf Girl: A Memoir of the Cultural Revolution,* Ji-Li Jiang. A compelling memoir of a girl's gradual disillusionment with communism.
66. *A Step from Heaven,* An Na. Young Ju must make many adjustments as her family moves from Korea to America.
67. *Under the Feet of Jesus,* Helena Maria Viramontes. The story of Mexican migrant farm workers, sort of a Latino version of *Grapes of Wrath.*

Fantasy/Science Fiction

68. *Dangerous Angels: The Weetzie Bat Books,* Francesca Lia Block. A book filled with magical realism and interesting characters, ghosts, and genies.
69. *Daughters of the Moon* (series), Lynne Ewing. Four teenagers are blessed with magical powers to battle the forces of evil.
70. *Ender's Game,* Orson Scott Card. Aliens have attacked Earth and the government turns to Ender to save the planet. A classic.
71. *The Giver,* Lois Lowry. In this futuristic story, Jonas is one of the chosen few who have the ability to remember the past.
72. *His Dark Materials* (trilogy): *The Golden Compass, The Subtle Knife,* and *The Amber Spyglass,* Philip Pullman. Fans of Harry Potter will like this series.
73. *Sabriel,* Garth Nix. Not for the faint of heart. Eighteen-year-old Sabriel sets off through the underworld to find her father.

74. *Sandry's Book (Circle of Magic 1)*, Tamora Pierce. Sandry and her magical friends use their powers when confronted by disaster.

Humor

75. *Calvin and Hobbes* (series), by Bill Watterson. Most high school students are unfamiliar with Calvin and Hobbes. This is a shame.
76. *The Far Side* (cartoon series), Gary Larson. A classroom favorite.
77. *Letters from a Nut*, Ted L. Nancy. Hilarious letters written to actual companies and the responses they elicit.
78. *Presumed Ignorant*, Leland Gregory. Did you know that in Santa Ana, California, it is illegal to swim on dry land? These and other goofy laws still on the books are found here.
79. *What's the Number for 911?*, Leland Gregory. Strange but true actual 911 calls.

Mystery

80. *Face on a Milk Carton*, Caroline Cooney. Fifteen-year-old Janie Johnson recognizes herself in a picture of a kidnapped three-year-old on a milk carton.
81. *Myron Bolitar* (series), Harlan Coben. Bolitar, a former professional basketball player and current sports agent, investigates crimes in the sporting world.
82. *Shades of Simon Gray*, Joyce McDonald. Sixteen-year-old Simon Gray falls into a coma after a mysterious accident, taking a secret with him.
83. *Stranger with My Face*, Lois Duncan. Laurie Stratton, seventeen, has a strange feeling someone is watching her.

Poetry

84. *Clean Slate: New and Selected Poems*, Daisy Zamora. Poetry from a revolutionary woman in Nicaragua, written from 1968 to 1993.
85. *Cool Salsa: Bilingual Poems on Growing Up Latino in the United States*, Lori Carlson. Poems for teens written in both English and Spanish.
86. *Gary Soto: New and Selected Poems*, Gary Soto. A collection of Soto's best poems.
87. *Immigrants in Our Own Land and Selected Early Poems*, Jimmy Santiago Baca. Baca, who wrote many of his poems in prison, is a favorite of my students.
88. *The Vintage Book of Contemporary American Poetry*, J. D. McClatchy. The work of sixty-five of our greatest poets.
89. *The Vintage Book of Contemporary World Poetry*, J. D. McClatchy. An indispensable, multicultural collection.
90. *What My Mother Doesn't Know*, Sonya Sones. A boy-crazy teen expresses her thoughts through her poetry.

War

91. *Black Hawk Down*, Mark Bowden. A nonfictional account of a disastrous military operation in Somalia.
92. *The Bomb*, Theodore Taylor. A teenager stands up to the government in an attempt to stop atomic testing on his island.
93. *Face of a Hero*, Louis Falstein. Intense depiction of air combat in World War II.

94. *Maus I and II,* Art Spiegelman. The story of Spiegelman's parents, who were swept up in the Holocaust. Told in serious comic book form.

95. *Not Even My Name,* Theo Halo. The nonfictional account of Turkish genocide, where three million people lost their lives.

96. *The Road from Home: The Story of an Armenian Girl,* David Kherdian. About the 1915 genocide in Armenia.

97. *Shrapnel in the Heart,* by Laura Palmer. A heart-wrenching visit to the Vietnam Memorial Wall, complete with vignettes about a number of soldiers memorialized there.

98. *The Things They Carried,* Tim O'Brien. A series of vignettes that accurately captures the American experience in Vietnam.

99. *Voices from Vietnam,* Barry Denenberg. The story of the Vietnam War as told through primary source documents and firsthand recollections.

100. *War Letters: Extraordinary Correspondence from American Wars,* Andrew Carroll. One hundred fifty letters from the front, spanning 130 years of warfare, from the Civil War to Bosnia.

101. *We Wish to Inform You That Tomorrow We Will Be Killed with Our Families: Stories From Rwanda,* Philip Gourevitch. Genocide in Rwanda took the lives of 800,000 people in 1994. This is an unflinching examination of the world's inaction while nearly a million people were killed.

Appendix C

Monthly Bulletin Board Ideas to Promote Reading

September: Reading Progress Chart

Every year I have my students record their reading progress on charts displayed in the classroom. Some teachers count pages or words; I prefer to count time spent reading. A slow reader who reads for twenty minutes receives the same credit as a fast reader, even though the fast reader may have read more words. I'm trying to build fluency in my slower readers, so in essence, I credit effort only.

Early in September I type the names of my students onto a spreadsheet. Next to each name is a series of boxes, each box representing five hours of reading (see Appendix K). I take this sheet to a copy center and have it enlarged into poster size. Every time a student completes five hours of reading, he or she places a star in the box, providing a visual of reading progress. (Stars or small stickers can be purchased in bulk at office supply stores.) I am still amused that even the toughest seniors, who come from some rough neighborhoods, radiate pride when they place gold stars next to their name.

When a student has read one million words (sixty hours of reading—see chart on page 178), I place his or her photograph in the center of a cutout star (I use a digital camera in class) and, using fishing line, hang it from the ceiling. I want everyone to see my reading stars.

October: Why We Read Hard Stuff

I want students to know that even proficient readers have trouble reading when asked to read something unfamiliar. This does not mean we give up when confronted with difficult text. It means we have to bear down and learn to read the hard stuff. (As much as I'd like to, I can't ignore that tax form every April.)

Somehow, students think teachers are expert readers of everything—that all text comes easy to us. We need to let students see us struggle with text. One of my favorite assignments is to have students bring to class reading material they think I will have trouble with. I then read—and think—aloud to model to them what an active reader does when confused. I have the students chart my strategies as I read and think aloud.

A bulletin board collage of all the different hard things we must read reinforces the idea that we are lifelong readers, that we never stop learning how to read, and that the more we practice reading difficult materials the better we will get at it.

November: I Didn't Know That!

At the beginning of October, I ask students to make notes of some of the things they are learning while they read at home. They begin the month knowing I will ask them at the end of the month to select the single most interesting thing they have learned through the month's reading. Come Halloween, we verbally snake around the room, with every student sharing a one-sentence summary of the most interesting thing he or she learned while reading. The students are immersed in interesting knowledge.

Next, I give every student a five-by-seven-inch blank index card. For homework they are asked to illustrate their knowledge, either literally or symbolically. They need to decorate the card in some way that expresses the knowledge they learned. Underneath the card they write a one-sentence caption explaining the interesting thing they learned. This becomes a bulletin board collage under the caption, "I Didn't Know That!"

December: Books Recommended by Students

It is one thing for a teacher to stand in front of the class and recommend books. But eventually, students might listen more closely to book recommendations if these recommendations come from their peers. To encourage book talk between students, I ask them to fill out a "Books Recommended by Students Form" (see Appendix E). Along with the written information provided by the student on the form, students can download an image of the book's cover. Form and cover are stapled together on a bulletin board (headed with the same title as the students' form). After the bulletin board fills up, I take down the recommendations and the class starts over. This bulletin board may be kept throughout the school year. At the end of the year I take all the recommendations and bind them in a booklet for next year's students.

January: Words of Wisdom

Halfway through the school year I ask students to think about everything they have read and to choose the wisest thing anyone has said. (This works better when students keep "Wisdom Logs" while they are reading.) Their selections can originate from fictional characters or real people. I give each student an index card or strip of cash register tape to write their chosen words of wisdom and to include the attribution. Before posting them, we go around the room and everyone reads his or her line (without any commentary). We then create a wisdom bulletin board. Now when kids stare blankly off into space you know they are at least reading something wise!

February: Words We Love

Students are not given enough time to discuss words. During February, have students keep a list of the most puzzling, funny, interesting, perplexing words they come across in their reading. In small groups, have each student share his or her word of the month. Give each student an index card, and for homework, have them decorate their card with their selected word. Ask them to make sure that the decorations help express the meaning of the words. These cards can become the basis of an interesting word wall.

March: The Hundred Greatest Novels of All Time?

In 1998 the Modern Library asked readers to identify the best novels of all time. Nearly a quarter of a million people voted. Create a bulletin board with this list on the left-hand side (obtain the list at www.randomhouse.com/modernlibrary/100 best/novels/html). Ask students to consider which of their favorite books have been overlooked. (Three books from L. Ron Hubbard and none from William Styron? Come on!) To the right of the list, leave room for students to add titles they feel should not have been omitted. Include downloaded book jacket art if space permits. Who knows, with a little encouragement maybe they will read one of these over spring break.

April: It's a Wacky World!

I try to encourage my students to read the daily newspaper. I do so by sharing with them strange but true newspaper stories. I collect them and share one a week with the students. A good source for these is *Jay Leno's Police Blotter: Real Life Crime Headlines*. (My favorite headline: "Would-be Robber Calls 911 for Help: Man Needed Way Out of Locked Bank After Breaking In.") I encourage students to bring me strange but true stories. I add them to my own and make a bulletin board collage with them. This shows students that reading the newspaper is fun as well as educational.

May: Show, Don't Tell

In May, we celebrate the craft of writing. Each student is given an index card and asked to search for the best descriptive passage he or she has read this year. On the appointed date, we read many of these out loud. It is powerful to hear snippets of beautiful writing being read aloud. When finished, students make a collage of beautiful writing on the bulletin board.

June: The Book of the Year! The Nominees Are . . .

At the end of our year together, students are asked to choose the best book they have read during the year and write a note to next year's class about why they should read this book. On the bulletin board I generate a list of the top-vote-getting books.

Appendix D

Book Donation Label

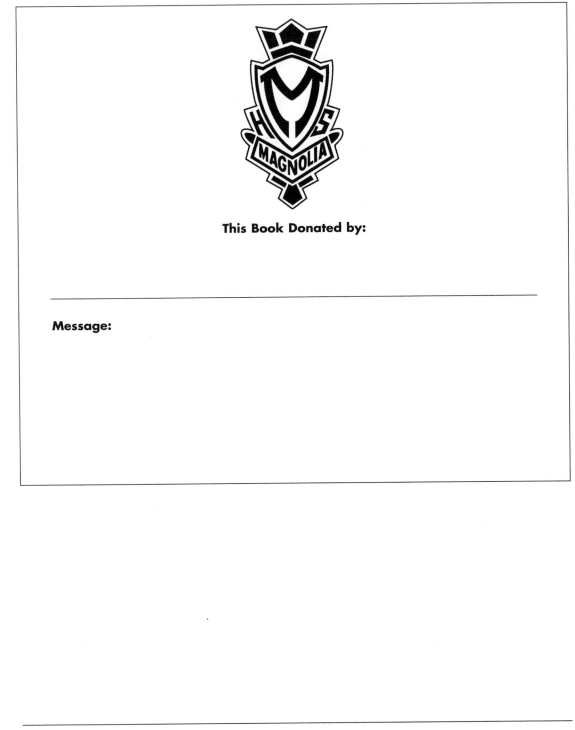

This Book Donated by:

_____

Message:

Appendix E

Books Recommended by Students Form

I recommend . . .

[image of book cover]

Title:

Author:

Where This Book Can Be Found:

Who Would Like This Book? Why?

Recommended by: **Period:**

Reading Reasons: Motivational Mini-Lessons for Middle and High School. Kelly Gallagher. Copyright © 2003. Stenhouse Publishers.

Appendix F

Parent Classroom Library Letter

Dear Parent(s),

Reading is a central focus in my classroom, and as we begin a new school year I would like to share some thoughts about reading with you.

Reading is a skill. The only way to get better at reading is to read—this holds true for excellent readers as well as reluctant readers. With this in mind, my goal is for your son or daughter to read two million words this school year. For the average student, two million words a year translates to forty minutes of reading every day. I will do my best to motivate your student to read academically as well as for fun. Some of the reading will be assigned, but your son or daughter will have opportunities to select his or her own books to be read independently.

To help your child reach the two-million-word goal, I have worked hard to develop my own classroom library. This library is available to any student who wants to choose a book to be read recreationally. Research shows that availability of books is a major motivating factor in getting teens to read. Students who are surrounded by books at school and at home read more. Students who read more, read better. I have found that having my own classroom library has dramatically increased the amount of reading my students do.

As a parent myself, I want you to know I am sensitive to having appropriate reading material in my classroom library. That said, what is considered "appropriate" may vary from one parent to another. Some parents do not mind their child reading Stephen King; other parents object to the horror genre. Please be aware that the selections in my classroom library, just like any public library, range from elementary-level to university-level reading material. As a parent, I ask you to remain aware throughout the year to the books your child has chosen to read and assist in gauging appropriateness.

Rest assured the books in my classroom library are never assigned. They are checked out on a voluntary basis only. Some students use my library a lot; others find books elsewhere. Any student who checks books out of my library is asked to have a parent or guardian sign below indicating that this classroom library letter has been read and understood.

My conference period is sixth period, from 1:45 to 2:40. If you have any questions, comments, or concerns, please feel free to contact me at XXX-XXXX. Let's get reading!

Sincerely,
Kelly Gallagher
English teacher, Magnolia High School

_____Yes, I have read this letter, and my son or daughter has permission to use Mr. Gallagher's classroom library.

_____No, I would prefer that my son or daughter not have access to Mr. Gallagher's classroom library.

Parent signature _____ Date _____

Parent of _____ Period _____

Appendix G

Books Read by the Magnolia High School Faculty Book Club

2002–2003

80. *Woodcuts of Women*, Dagoberto Gilb
79. *Empire Falls*, Richard Russo
78. *Traveling Mercies*, Anne Lamott
77. *Peace Like a River*, Leif Enger
76. *The Corrections*, Jonathan Franzen
75. *The Scandalous Summer of Sissy LeBlanc*, Loraine Despres

2001–2002

74. *And Still We Rise*, Miles Corwin
73. *Seabiscuit: An American Legend*, Laura Hillenbrand
72. *The Blind Assassin*, Margaret Atwood
71. *Fast Food Nation*, Eric Schlosser
70. *Beachcombing for a Shipwrecked God*, Joe Coomer
69. *The Amazing Adventures of Kavalier and Clay*, Michael Chabon
68. *Endurance: Shackleton's Incredible Voyage*, Alfred Lansing
67. *Me Talk Pretty One Day*, David Sedaris

2000–2001

66. *Bad Haircut: Stories of the 70's*, Tom Perrotta
65. *A Heartbreaking Work of Staggering Genius*, Dave Eggers
64. *Farmer*, Jim Harrison
63. *The Lives of a Cell*, Lewis Thomas
62. *Plainsong*, Kent Haruf
61. *L.A. Requiem*, Robert Crais
60. *The Story of a Million Years*, David Huddle
59. *The Poisonwood Bible*, Barbara Kingsolver
58. *Zodiac*, Robert Graysmith

1999–2000

57. *The Hours*, Michael Cunningham
56. *Ship of Gold in the Deep Blue Sea*, Gary Kinder
55. *Fade Away*, Harlan Coben
54. *Face of a Hero*, Louis Falstein
53. *The Cider House Rules*, John Irving
52. *Einstein's Dreams*, Alan Lightman

51. *Memoirs of a Geisha,* Arthur Golden
50. *The Hot Zone,* Richard Preston
49. *The Reader,* Bernard Schlink

1998–1999

48. *Victims of Justice,* John Frisbie
47. *Animal Husbandry,* Laura Zigman
46. *The Measure of Our Days,* Jerome Groopman
45. *Wobegon Boy,* Garrison Keillor
44. *One Flew over the Cuckoo's Nest,* Ken Kesey
43. *Lucky You,* Carl Haisson
42. *Cold Mountain,* Charles Frazier

1997–1998

41. *Into Thin Air,* Jon Krakauer
40. *The Killing Season,* Miles Corwin
39. *The Names of the Dead,* Stewart O'Nan
38. *Farewell, I'm Bound to Leave You,* Fred Chappell
37. *Montana 1948,* Larry Watson
36. *Of Love and Dust,* Ernest J. Gaines
35. *A Good Scent from a Strange Mountain,* R. O. Butler
34. *A Civil Action,* Jonathan Harr
33. *The Giant's House,* Susan McCracken

1996–1997

32. *Floaters,* Joseph Wambaugh
31. *A Confederacy of Dunces,* John Kennedy Toole
30. *The Book of Ruth,* Jane Hamilton
29. *Suburban Guerrillas,* Joseph Freda
28. *Under the Feet of Jesus,* Helena Maria Viramontes
27. *Bailey's Café,* Gloria Naylor
26. *The Magic of Blood,* Dagoberto Gilb

1995–1996

25. *The Day After Tomorrow,* Allan Folsom
24. *Those Same Long Bones,* Gwendolyn Parker
23. *The Stone Diaries,* Carol Shields
22. *A Long Line of Dead Men,* Lawrence Block
21. *Snow Falling on Cedars,* David Guterson
20. *Stones from the River,* Ursula Hegi
19. *In the Lake of the Woods,* Tim O'Brien
18. *So Far from God,* Ana Castillo

1994–1995

17. *The Celestine Prophesy,* James Redfield
16. *A Lesson Before Dying,* Ernest J. Gaines
15. *I Am One of You Forever,* Fred Chappell
14. *The Angle of Repose,* Wallace Stegner
13. *Smila's Sense of Snow,* Peter Hoeg
12. *The Shipping News,* E. Annie Proulx
11. *What's Eating Gilbert Grape?,* Peter Hedges
10. *The Bean Trees,* Barbara Kingsolver
 9. *Jazz,* Toni Morrison

1993–1994

8. *A Thousand Acres,* Jane Smiley
7. *Bastard Out of Carolina,* Dorothy Allison
6. *The Things They Carried,* Tim O'Brien
5. *The Children of Men,* P. D. James
4. *Loves Music, Loves to Dance,* Mary Higgins Clark
3. *The Remains of the Day,* Kazuo Ishiguro
2. *Mama Day,* Gloria Naylor
1. *The Joy Luck Club,* Amy Tan

Appendix H

Reading Log

Date	B	N	M	O	Material Read/Explanation	Minutes Read	Total Hours Read

B = book   M = magazine   N = newspaper   O = other

Appendix I

Reading Record

Works read by _____ Period _____

			Title of Work Read	Author	Genre	Date Finished	Date Abandoned	No. of pages read	Rating

This box to be completed in June
Total hours read this year _____
Total works read this year _____
Total words read this year _____

Title of Work Read	Author	Genre	Date Finished	Date Abandoned	No. of pages read	Rating

Genres   Biography   Sports   Humor   Fantasy   Poetry
Horror   Nonfiction   Drama   Romance   Science Fiction
Short Story   Mystery   Classical Fiction   Historical Fiction   Contemporary Fiction

Appendix J

Magazine Check-Out

Please Return Your Magazine Tomorrow

Your Name	Today's Date	Name of Magazine	Date of Magazine

Appendix K

Classroom Time Chart

| Name | | | | | | | | | | | | |

Name	Hours Read											
	5	10	15	20	25	30	35	40	45	50	55	60
1												
2												
3												
4												
5												
6												
7												
8												
9												
10												
11												
12												
13												
14												
15												
16												
17												
18												
19												
20												
21												
22												
23												
24												
25												
26												
27												
28												
29												
30												
31												
32												
33												
34												
35												
36												
37												
38												
39												
40												

BIBLIOGRAPHY

Anderson, Richard C., Paul T. Wilson, and Linda G. Fielding. 1988. "Growth in Reading and How Children Spend Their Time Outside of School." *Reading Research Quarterly* 23: 285–303.

Atwell, Nancie. 1998. *In the Middle: Writing, Reading, and Learning with Adolescents,* 2d ed. Portsmouth, NH: Heinemann-Boynton/Cook.

"The Big Payoff: Educational Attainment and Synthetic Estimates of Work-Life Earnings." 2000. U.S. Census Bureau, Current Population Surveys.

Bronfenbrenner, Urie, Peter McClelland, Elaine Wethington, Phyllis Moen, and Stephen J. Ceci. 1996. *The State of Americans: This Generation and the Next.* New York: Free Press.

Burke, Kenneth. 1968. "Psychology and Form." In *Counter-Statement.* 2d ed. Berkeley: University of California Press.

"Education May Protect Against Alzheimer's Disease and Other Forms of Dementia." 2000. Chicago: Alzheimer's Disease and Related Disorders Association.

English Language and Composition, English Literature and Composition Course Description E. May 2003, May 2004. New York: The College Board.

Ericson, Bonnie O., ed. 2001. *Teaching Reading in High School English Classes.* Urbana, IL: National Council Teachers of English.

Feathers, Karen. 1993. *Infotext: Reading and Learning.* Toronto: Pippin.

Grant, Jim, and Char Forsten. 1999. *If You're Riding a Horse and It Dies, Get Off.* Peterborough, NH: Crystal Springs.

Haycock, Kati. 2001. "Closing the Achievement Gap." *Educational Leadership* 58, no. 6: 28–31.

Hayes, Donald P., and Margaret G. Ahrens. 1988. "Vocabulary Simplification for Children: A Special Case for 'Motherese.'" *Journal of Child Language* 15: 401, 403.

Hillenbrand, Laura. 2001. *Seabiscuit: An American Legend.* New York: Randon House.

Kohn, Alfie. 1998. *Punished by Rewards.* Boston: Houghton Mifflin.

Krashen, Stephen. 1993. *The Power of Reading: Insights from the Research.* Edgewood, CO: Libraries Unlimited.

Lamott, Anne. 1994. *Bird by Bird: Some Instructions on Writing and Life.* New York: Anchor.

Lansing, Alfred. 1959. *Endurance: Shackleton's Incredible Voyage.* New York: Carroll & Graf.

A League of Their Own. 1992. Columbia/Tristar Studios.

Leno, Jay. 1994. *Jay Leno's Police Blotter: Real-Life Crime Headlines.* Kansas City, MO: Andrews and McMeel.

McQuillan, Jeff. 1998. *The Literacy Crisis: False Claims, Real Solutions.* Portsmouth, NH: Heinemann.

Murnane, Richard J., and Frank Levy. 1996. *Teaching the New Basic Skills: Principles for Educating Children to Thrive in a Changing Economy.* New York: Free Press.

National Assessment of Educational Progress (NAEP). 1997. "Reading Assessment in the Nation's Fourth- and Eighth-Grade Classrooms." *NAEP Facts* 2, no. 3: 1–5.

National Center for Educational Statistics (NCES). 1994. *Data Compendium for the NAEP 1992 Reading Assessment of the Nation and the States.* Washington DC: U.S. Department of Education.

Neergaard, Lauran. 2001. "Memory a Matter of Brains and Brawn: Mental, Physical Exertion Needed to Preserve the Mind." Associated Press. *San Francisco Chronicle,* 24 July 2000.

Official Rules of Softball: 2002. 2002. Oklahoma City: Amateur Softball Association of America.

Olson, Carol Booth. 2003. *The Reading/Writing Connection: Strategies for Teaching and Learning in the Secondary Classroom.* Boston: Allyn and Bacon.

Palmer, Parker J. 1998. *The Courage to Teach: Exploring the Inner Landscape of a Teacher's Life.* San Francisco: Jossey-Bass.

Paul, Terrence. 1996. *Patterns of Reading Practice.* Institute for Academic Excellence.

Readence, John E., Thomas W. Bean, and R. Scott Baldwin. 2000. *Content Area Literacy: An Integrated Approach.* Dubuque, IA: Kendall/Hunt.

"Reading Assessment in the Nation's Fourth- and Eighth-Grade Classrooms." 1997. National Center for Education Statistics, Vol. 2, No. 3. United States Department of Education.

Reading/Language Arts Framework for California Public Schools: Kindergarten Through Grade Twelve. 1999. Sacramento: CDE Press.

Real SAT II: Subject Tests. 1998. Forrester Center, WV: The College Board.

Schlosser, Eric. 2001. *Fast Food Nation: The Dark Side of the American Meal.* New York: Harper Collins.

Seipp, Michele, Sandra Lindberg, and Keith Curry Lance. 2002. "Book Displays Increase Fiction Circulation Over 90%, Non-Fiction Circulation 25%." *Fast Facts.* ED3/110.10. No. 184. Denver: Colorado Department of Education.

Ten Real SATs. 2000. New York: College Entrance Examination Board.

Trelease, Jim. 2001. *The Read-Aloud Handbook.* New York: Penguin.

U.S. Department of Commerce, Bureau of the Census. 1998. *Current Population Report: Educational Attainment in the United States.* Washington, DC.

U.S. Department of Education. 2000. *The Early Childhood Longitudinal Study, Kindergarten Class of 1998–1999.* Washington, DC.